Once-Told Tales of Worcester County

D0967192

Once-Told Tales of Worcester County

ALBERT B. SOUTHWICK

PUBLISHED BY DATABOOKS

A Division of Tatnuck Bookseller & Sons, Inc.
Worcester, MA
1994

Library of Congress Catalog Card Number 94-71907
ISBN 0-9636277-5-9

Originally published by Worcester Telegram & Gazette, Worcester, Massachusetts, 1985.

To order additional quantities of this book or More Once-Told Tales of Worcester County or any other books on Worcester, Massachusetts
DATABOOKS
Mail Order & Sales Desk
335 Chandler Street
Worcester, MA 01602-3441
FAX 508—756-9425
1-800-642-6657 (USA)
Internet: databooks@delphi.com

Cover
Downtown Worcester in 1913-14, looking south from Front Street near Harrington Corner. The Park Building, opened in 1914, is not yet completed. Across Main Street is the Jonas C. Clark building, rented by Denholm and McKay's Boston Store. The old Flatiron Building can be seen at the junction of Main and Southbridge Street, in front of the old Post Office building

To Shirley

Acknowledgments

MANY PERSONS have helped me with this book. I particularly want to give credit to William Wallace, Dorothy Gleason and Mark Savolis of the Worcester Historical Museum, Georgia Bumgardner of the American Antiquarian Society, Nancy Gaudette of the Worcester Public Library, E.B. Luce Corp., Robert Wilson, Philip Davis, Sharon Carter of the Telegram and Gazette library and the Rev. Richard D. McGrail of The Catholic Free Press. I appreciate their generous assistance very much. I also want to thank Sid McKeen for coming up with the title for the book.

Albert B. Southwick

Contents

Chapters

Chapters

Preface

HISTORY TAKES ITS LUMPS. Matthew Arnold saw history as a "huge Mississippi of falsehoods." Napoleon is said to have described it as "a fable agreed upon." Henry Ford called it "more or less bunk."

But where would we be without it?

If history is for school children, then we should all sit at the other end of that log and listen. For we learn there something about who and where we came from, what works and what doesn't work, where lie the joys of life, and its sorrows.

Worcester County is rich in history, and ankle-deep in historians. The Rev. Peter Whitney was among the first to write the record — if not right the record — in 1793. He was followed by such worthies as William Lincoln, Charles G. Washburn, Charles Nutt and John Nelson — the latter two having been newspaper practitioners of distinction, Nutt with the Worcester Daily Spy, Nelson with the Worcester Telegram and The Evening Gazette.

Enter Albert B. Southwick. He writes as a trained historian and a concerned observer of the world. He grew up in Leicester on a farm that had been in his family for generations. He was graduated from Clark University, spent four years in the Navy, earned his master's degree in American history at Clark and undertook advanced studies at Brown University.

For two years, 1950-52, he was a civilian historian in Germany for the U.S. Army. He went on to newspaper work, first at the Providence Journal and for the past 33 years at the Worcester Telegram and Gazette. As an editorial writer for 15 years and chief editorial writer for 18 years, he has watched, studied and commented on the great issues of our times.

Those words — "great issues" — can mislead. For Mr. Southwick knows the homely truth: History is made by people and great issues arise from small events. He has never lost interest in the world of home and work and commmunity, where people live their lives. He wrote for the Worcester Telegram a classic series of "Down on the Farm" columns. A group of his editorials on nature were collected under the title of "New England Around the Year." For his home town, he helped create a Leicester Room at the junior college, rich with historic documents.

At various moments in his own colorful history, Mr. Southwick has been a bomber pilot, opera librettist, Savoyard, Shakespearean, member of Phi Beta Kappa and recipient of many journalistic awards.

Yet he always comes back to history. It fascinates him and he fascinates us as he tells the tales of our beginnings.

There is no pedantry here. This historian does not put himself forward as George Bancroft, or Whitney, Nutt or Nelson. He tells about people and their dreams, where those dreams took them and where they have brought us. Many of these accounts of life in Worcester County were first written for the Worcester Telegram or The Evening Gazette. We present them here along with material not previously published.

When all the tales are told, they form a brilliant mosaic of Worcester County in its youthful years.

This volume blends enjoyment with fact, insight with pleasure. It brings freshness to history. It rescues the word from its critics.

We at the Worcester Telegram and The Evening Gazette are delighted to join with Albert Southwick in bringing you this volume.

Robert C. Achorn, Publisher,
Worcester Telegram
and The Evening Gazette

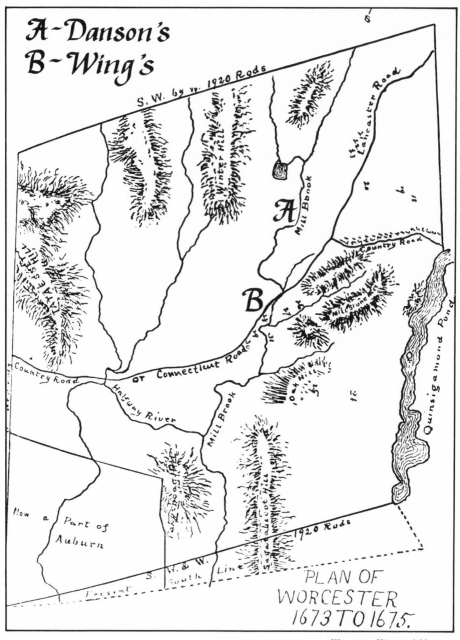

This map, drawn by Worcester historian Ellery B. Crane years ago, shows Worcester as it may have looked in 1685. The path marked "Country Road or Connecticut Road" is the current Route 9. "Lancaster Road" is now Lincoln Street. "A" marks the approximate location of George Danson's property. "B" marks John Wing's property.

Chapter 1

Worcester's First Lawsuit

IT WAS A TENSE MOMENT. The two men confronted each other and exchanged insults and accusations. One brandished an ax as he shouted: "You rogue, get off my land!"

"In Boston you called me a black dog. I'm not afraid of you," retorted the second man. A fight seemed likely but was averted at the last moment. Worcester, which had no lawyer, no courthouse, no town hall, about 25 people, about six houses and only a few paths winding through the woods, was headed for its first lawsuit.

The time was March 1685. The place was somewhere between what is now Indian Lake and Lincoln Square. The men were John Wing and George Danson, both of Boston. They both had bought land in the new settlement and were arguing over boundaries and water rights on Mill Brook, which ran from North Pond (Indian Lake) southward through the settlement and into the Blackstone River.

Mill Brook now runs mainly underground in huge aqueducts. But in those days it was the chief potential source of power for the new village. Somewhere near Wheaton Square, Wing was building dams, a sawmill and a gristmill. He needed to control the water rights at North Pond to ensure a proper flow of water for his waterwheels. But Danson also had been awarded some lots along Mill Brook. He and David Fiske, surveyor, had been surveying the bounds when Wing and his friends accosted them on that spring day. There were more confrontations during the spring and fall. According to the case records of Danson Vs. Wing, filed in Middlesex Court in December 1685, "Wing & confederators did on the 2nd of this instant October violently set upon & assault the Plaintiff as he was laying out some parcels of land at the Towne of Worcester" smashing the surveyor chain, tearing up stakes and driving Danson and the surveyor from the scene.

Danson and Wing. Who were they?

In the old records of Boston, Capt. John Wing is listed as a "mariner." He was one of the founders of the Old South Church in 1669, an officer in the Artillery

1

Company and keeper of a tavern. At one point, the tavern had a room for "a man to show tricks in," but the Boston authorities quickly put a stop to that.

Wing became interested in the new settlement of Worcester in 1684, and by March 1685 was busily building his house somewhere near Lincoln Square, perhaps where the Memorial Auditorium stands.

Wing's hewn log house may have been one of the garrisons for the tiny settlement. It was there that the settlers would go if the Indians attacked. Wing also may have kept a tavern, although the original tavern license was given to Nathaniel Henchman (or Hinchman), the 21-year-old son of Daniel Henchman. The older Henchman was in charge of parceling out and selling the lots to the proprietors. He was the first developer in Worcester.

George Danson was a "loaf bread baker," a Quaker who had twice been whipped in Boston for attending Quaker meetings. In 1674, he had been fined 40 shillings "for doing servile work on the Lords day." By 1685, he was an old man and reasonably prosperous. Why he decided to make the move to Worcester is a puzzle, but perhaps he thought the new settlement would be farther removed from the intolerant church authorities of Boston.

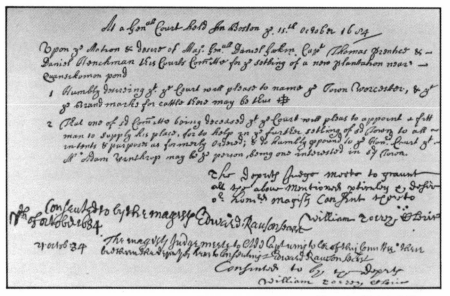

Worcester Historical Museum

The petition of Daniel Gookin and his associates on Oct. 18, 1684, asked the Massachusetts General Court " please to name the town Worcester" and set brand marks for the settlers' cattle.

2

Daniel Henchman seems not to have fully appreciated the importance of water rights. He sold Wing land on the west side of Mill Brook, from a spot north of what is now Lincoln Square part way upstream to North Pond (Indian Lake). Wing obviously understood that he would have exclusive water rights to North Pond. But when Danson bought the rest of the land along the brook, he assumed he had water rights, too.

Henchman was not a profile in courage. He bent this way and that as Danson and Wing pressed their claims. When it became clear that most of the settlers backed Wing, Henchman did, too, "to hinder the town from buzing about my eares." He assured Wing that he never wanted to grant the land to Danson in the first place, but "he would have none other."

The case was heard in the court at Charlestown. Almost every person in town journeyed to Charlestown, either as witnesses or observers. They were overwhelmingly in favor of Wing. But the court was presented an affidavit from Daniel Henchman, then lying on his deathbed back in Worcester:

Worcester Octo 5th. 85

Received of mr. Danson five pounds ten shilings for eleven Lotts in Worcester and nine Lotts which he bought of severall persons and have delivered me the assignments of them in all twenty Lotts And he chose his planting Lotts to be Layed out next Capt Wings planting Lotts which land piched uppon him by I have not disposed of to any other person or promised the same uppon any other account to any: or was it in my power So to do And the molestation given him by Capt. Wing is unjust This I testifie as one at the Point of deth the Riteous God knoweth I speak the truth.

D. Henchman
Witness David ffiske
Nathaniel Henchman

In July 1686, the committee appointed by the government in Boston to confirm land claims in Worcester granted Danson full and clear title to his land. But it stipulated that Danson should not "erect any corne mil or Saw mill upon the mil Brook . . ." Wing got what he wanted after all.

It was all for nought. In 1690, the Indians again began to threaten the outlying settlements. In 1695, Samuel Leonard Jr., son of Worcester's constable, was kidnapped from his home. For two years, he traveled with the Indians along with other captives. They escaped in April 1697 after killing a sleeping brave with a tomahawk.

But young Leonard never came back to Worcester to live. His family, along with most of the others, had left for safer places. On March 22, 1699, the name of

3

Worcester was dropped from the list of frontier towns. By 1702, only Diggory Sergeant and his family remained in the ghostly settlement.

The Indians killed Diggory just before an expedition arrived to bring the family out of the doomed village with its abandoned houses. His wife and youngest child were slaughtered on the trail west. Two of the children remained with the Indians for the rest of their lives. The other two survived and escaped, but never came back to Worcester.

Not until 1713 did Jonas Rice return to his farm on Union Hill. That was the start of the third settlement, the one that was to last.

George Danson died in 1692, leaving 500 acres of land in Worcester to his wife. His estate included a considerable amount of merchandise and dry goods.

John Wing died in 1702, leaving his son, Cord, his "Frame House and land in Worcester with four hundred acres on the west side of the river & running to the north pond & northerly to the top of Prospect Hill." He apparently had acquired all of Danson's land after Danson's death. His estate in Boston was even larger.

Three hundred years have passed and neither Wing nor Danson has a single, solitary monument or plaque in Worcester. Only one short driveway on the Worcester Polytechnic Institute campus bears John Wing's name. Danson has been forgotten.

Shouldn't somebody or some organization — maybe the Worcester County Bar Association — do something to keep their memory green?

After all, as the first litigants in Worcester history, they established a lasting precedent.

4

Chapter 2

Leicester's Hermit — An Unsolved Mystery

THE MAN CUT OFF FOR YEARS from civilization is a staple of fiction and legend. Robinson Crusoe, Rip Van Winkle, Andrew Selkirk, Ben Gunn, Daniel Boone — figures like these linger in the imagination.

Leicester has its own dim legend — Arthur Carey, the hermit of Carey Hill, where the Leicester water tanks now stand. Who was he? Where did he come from? Did he really keep a fire burning in his cave for 40 years? Where did he go when he walked out of town that day in 1730 or thereabouts, supposedly headed for Boston? Why did he vanish forever, leaving his claim to 550 acres of the best land in town? Did he really have a big hoard of gold coins stashed in his cave? What is fact and what is fiction?

One fact about Carey seems certain: He was the first white settler in Leicester, predating all others by 25 years or more. An old history of Worcester County notes that, long before the other settlers arrived in town, Carey "went thither and digged a cave in the side of this hill, and lived there as a hermit many years, while that part of the country was in its wilderness state." In 1699, a scouting party discovered him, much to everybody's surprise. Then and there began the legend of Arthur Carey.

The tract called Towtaid was bought for 15 English pounds from the Indians on Jan. 27, 1686 (old style) by a group of Boston investors. It included all of what is now Leicester, part of Spencer, part of Auburn and most of Paxton — a huge parcel of land.

As was the practice in those days, the proprietors planned to sell part of the land to settlers, holding the other part for future sale when land values would have increased. But, because of Indian unrest and a lack of willing settlers, not until 1699 did the first scouting and surveying parties arrive.

If Carey was upset about this intrusion on his solitary tranquillity, he did not show any hostility. Although he had "almost forgotten human speech" and required several days before he could carry on a conversation, he came to talk freely, according to the accounts. He said that he was born in Ireland and had

5

Worcester Telegram & Gazette

The only white man in Worcester County in 1675 was Ephraim Curtis, who lived near what is now Lincoln Plaza on Lincoln Street. Arthur Carey claimed he had met Curtis at about that time. Curtis died at age 92 after surviving Indian attacks, wilderness hazards, rattlesnakes and other menaces. The above depiction is by Brierly, an artist who did a series of sketches of Worcester history for the Worcester Telegram a generation ago.

come to the wilderness to have "peace of mind." He spoke bitterly of the British and said his father had been a soldier who had fought against Cromwell. Only later did anyone come to doubt Carey's story or suspect that there may have been other reasons for Carey's decision to move beyond the reach of the law.

Carey said that he had left Boston years before in the dead of night and traveled westward through the forest paths for days. As he walked around the end of a "long pond" he met another white man, armed with a musket and dressed in furs.

The man's name was Ephraim Curtis, he said.

With that mention of Curtis, Carey's account became more believable. Curtis was the first settler in Worcester. He was there as early as 1673, before King Philip's War. The scouting party had heard of Curtis. It seemed likely that Carey had met him at least 25 years before.

In 1921, the Worcester Telegram did a comprehensive article on Carey, trying to separate fact from fiction. According to that account:

"He dug his cave into the hillside with sharpened pine splinters and when he got it about 10 feet deep, he fashioned rude supports for the roof out of fallen trees. He had only an axe and a very few utensils, all that he carried on his back on the long walk through the wilderness from Boston . . . Carey made bows and arrows and managed to snare rabbits and shoot deer and wild fowl enough to keep alive, but his methods were ruder and cruder than those of the Indians who at least had a few of the necessities of life."

He kept a fire burning continually and said he had not let it go out for 40 years. Sticks, logs and brush were piled in profusion around the mouth of the cave. He had no flint and steel, no guns. He eagerly traded some of his furs for a gun and powder and shot. But he said that he never had any trouble with the Indians, even during the massacre time of King Philip's War. He had a set of crude soapstone dishes that he got in trade from the Indians.

That is one picture of Arthur Carey, the hermit in the wilderness. There is another picture even more puzzling.

After 1714, the settlers began to trickle into the new settlement. Carey, according to one account, disappeared into the wilderness, presumably seeking the solitude and quiet that he was losing.

But then came the time for the parceling out of lots to the settlers. Lo and behold, who came out of the woods — or somewhere — but Arthur Carey. He laid claim to 550 acres of land surrounding his cave. But — most surprising to everyone — he paid for his land "in gold coins as shiny as if they came from the mint." At that time, coins of any sort, let alone gold, were so scarce as to be nonexistent in the outlying settlements.

7

It is a fact that Carey is listed on the records as one of the original settlers of Leicester. According to the Telegram account, he built a log cabin on his property — the first in town built by a white man.

Not much is known about Carey for the next few years, except that he was said to have paid for everything he bought with gold or silver coins.

And then, one day, reports say, he reappeared in Leicester for the last time, "dressed in clothes much better than the average settler could afford." He carried a gold-headed cane and was said to have had plenty of money. "He remarked that he was going to Worcester and thence to Boston. He was seen in Worcester where he was a guest at the Stearns Hotel. After his departure next morning by the post coach for Boston, he was never seen in Leicester again."

The years went by. On the assumption that Carey was dead, his 550 acres were parceled out to others, who probably worried about their land titles for years afterward. But he never came back.

His unexplained disappearance, his markedly changed circumstances, the gold coins, the fancy clothes, all nurtured many theories and legends in the years to come. One of the most popular was that he had been a pirate and had carried his stolen wealth deep into the wilderness where he would be safe from the law and from other predatory thieves. There were reports that, years before, Indians had told Capt. Daniel Gookin and the Rev. John Eliot about meeting a white man "burdened with a great pack on his back and carrying many shining pieces of frozen water that did not melt, but glimmered in the sun, and that he also had an immense store of round yellow metal that he kept hidden from his Redmen friends, even when he exchanged the pipe of peace at a neighborhood powwow." If there is any truth to that report, the Indians almost certainly were talking about Carey.

In later years, the legends grew fanciful. He had been one of the pirates who had sacked ships outside of Boston Harbor and had "sent the men and women on board to walk the plank before burning the ship." Or, even better, Carey and his band of brigands had been captured and sentenced to hang. He alone escaped, "released from a stone cell through pity of a jailer's daughter."

These tales about Arthur Carey enlivened many an evening before the roaring fireplaces in Leicester for a century afterward. At this late date, there is no way to disentangle the myth from the reality. The mystery of Carey remains as dark today as it was in 1725.

8

Chapter 3

Bloody Times in Old Rutland

RUTLAND IS NOW A QUIET, lovely place, an old New England town set high on a hill.

But it was not always peaceful. On one August day, the minister of the Congregational Church was slaughtered in broad daylight. On that same day, the church deacon saw two of his sons murdered and two more kidnapped and dragged off into the wilderness.

Almost one year later, three Rutland men were cut down in cold blood and another boy kidnapped. The terrified people of Rutland appealed to the authorities in Boston for protection.

The years 1723 and 1724 were the worst that Rutland has ever experienced. Rutland was one of the outpost settlements most exposed to Indian raids. To the north were forests, stretching all the way to Canada. The tiny settlement of Brookfield lay 10 miles to the west, almost a day's walk or ride through narrow trails. Holden lay almost as far to the south. The two dozen settlers on the high, wooded hills of Rutland were isolated, alone, cut off from even rudimentary civilization.

1722, the year that Rutland was settled, was a bad time to be on the edge of the wilderness. Led by their redoubtable chief, Gray Lock, and instigated by the French in Canada, the Abenaki and Waranoke Indians began to make forays against the English settlements. The Boston authorities ordered the Rutland settlers to build a fort around the house of the minister, the Rev. Joseph Willard. But forts were no defense against the sneak attacks launched by the wily Gray Lock. With no more than 10 or 15 braves, he would move silent as a shadow through the woods, picking off isolated settlers working in their fields.

In the summer of 1723, Gray Lock began his depredations. In early August, his band waylaid Northfield, killing two settlers and then disappearing into the forest before the stunned townsfolk could organize a pursuit. Gray Lock and his men moved swiftly. Shortly they were lurking in the forest around Rutland, looking for victims, which they soon found. Deacon Joseph Stevens, working

9

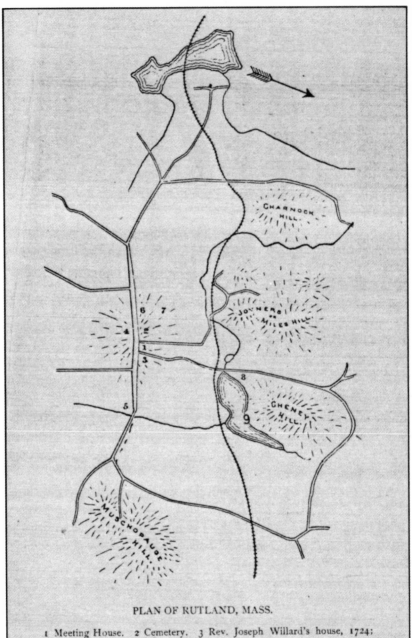

PLAN OF RUTLAND, MASS.

1 Meeting House. 2 Cemetery. 3 Rev. Joseph Willard's house, 1724; Muschopauge Hotel, 1885. 4 Capt. Sam'l Wright's house, 1724. 5 Lt. Simon Davis's house, 1724. 6 Dea. Joseph Stevens's House, 1724. 7 Where the Stevens boys were killed, 1723. 8 - 9 Both these spots are indicated on a plan by Dea. Reed as the place where Rev. Mr. Willard was killed, 9 being on the border of the ministry meadow.

10

alone in a field, all of a sudden heard shrieks and the dread Indian war cry. The Indians had waylaid his four sons, who were headed for the field to join their father. Stevens, horrified, saw the Indians slay two of his boys and then disappear into the woods with the other two as prisoners.

The Indians then apparently tried to waylay Simon Davis and his son, who were working in another field, but Davis, possibly because he heard the shouting from the Stevens place, was nowhere to be found. Gray Lock and his men moved on to Cheney Hill, where they came upon Rev. Willard coming back from a hunting trip.

The pastor did not turn the other cheek. As two Indians fired their guns at him, he fired back, severely wounding one, who may have died later. Then it was hand-to-hand combat. According to a man who said he witnessed the struggle, the doughty Willard was getting the better of his enemy when three other Indians rushed up and dispatched him with their tomahawks. The news story published in Boston said that he was "barbarously murdered" which meant he was scalped.

The bloody news from Northfield and Rutland spread throughout the settlements, causing some people to leave for safer locations nearer to Boston. Lt. Gov. William Dummer, in charge of security, was besieged with requests for soldiers from Northfield, Brookfield, Rutland, Groton, Dunstable and the other exposed places. Dummer did the best he could. Troops were sent out to protect the tiny settlements. Capt. Samuel Wright, in charge of protecting Rutland, wrote to Boston that he needed more men.

"It might be that we might have our Scout much biger Seven men being too Little to Range without our Town, from the Watchusett Hills on the Back Side of Ware River, & so to the Back side of Brookfield, which might be of tenn times the Service to these Towns, than this Scout can be, because these Scouts only goe in Small percels withn the Towns where we may be sure will come no Indians, Except One or two to Spie who go So private they cant be seen."

Wright's contingent was beefed up to 38 men, including some of the settlers. But that was not enough to forestall a second tragedy.

In the spring of 1724, Gray Lock and his warriors were again on the march. They knew the woods like a book and they traveled light. From the edge of the clearings they could study what the white men were doing. On Aug. 3, they fell on Rutland for a second time, surrounding five men and a boy working in a field. Uriah Ward, Joseph Wood and James Clark were killed and scalped. The boy, presumably kidnapped and probably slain, was never heard from again.

The second attack on Rutland alarmed the whole colony. The Boston authorities redoubled the troops and launched search expeditions. But not a single Indian was ever captured.

A letter to Dummer from Wright tells what the defenders were up against: "The Indians are among us, and have discovered themselves many times, and we have had several pursuits after them, and have been very vigilant in prosecuting all methods to come up with them by watching the swamps and lurking places, and by watching at nights in private places outside the garrisons; but they are so much like wolves that we cannot surprise them . . . We have now taken a method to hunt them with dogs and have started them out of their thickets twice, and see them run out, but at such a distance we could not come at them."

Those must have been fearful days for the 15 families who remained in Rutland. In times of peril, they would all sleep in the fort in the center of the village, probably near where the Rutland Fire Station now stands. When a family did spend the night in its crude log hut, the musket was always standing ready in a convenient place. The menacing sounds of the night — the howling of wolves was then common — must have been particularly frightening for the children, who had known the four Stevens boys — the two who had been slaughtered and the two, Phineas and Isaac, who had been kidnapped and abducted by the Indians to no one knew where. And also the boy, unnamed in the documents, who disappeared at the time of the latest Indian attack.

But although Indians occasionally were seen for several years afterward, there were no more tragedies visited upon Rutland. In December 1725, the colonial government signed a treaty of peace with the eastern Indians. Some of the settlers returned. By 1727, Rutland had 25 families.

And what about Phineas and Isaac Stevens, captured by the Indians on that grim summer day in 1723? With the dread memory of their slain brothers impressed in their minds, they stumbled through the woodland trails on the long journey to Canada. Little Isaac was only 4, and the Indians apparently considered killing him after a day or so. But Phineas, 17, guessing what they were talking about, lifted Isaac on his back and made it clear that he would carry the little boy and thus relieve them of any burden. They finally arrived in Canada and lived with the Indians.

Meanwhile their father, armed with a letter from Dummer, made the long journey to Canada and won the release of Phineas in 1724. Since Gray Lock had given Isaac to another tribe, it took another year to get him back. Isaac, by that time, had become attached to the Indian woman who cared for him and would willingly have stayed with the Indians for the rest of his life. That sometimes happened with white children brought up by Indians. But he returned to Rutland where he eventually married and had a large family.

Phineas, the older son, was to have an interesting career. He moved from Rutland to New Hampshire, and became prominent in public life. In 1749, he was commissioned by the governor of Massachusetts province to go to Canada and negotiate for the release of captives held by the Indians. He made several journeys for that purpose and successfully freed a number of prisoners, including one John Stark, later a general in the Revolution. To get Stark back, he traded the Indians a pony.

His father, Deacon Stevens, lived on for many years. Because he had been impoverished by the expenses of getting his sons back from Canada, collections were taken up for him in various churches. In 1732, the General Court granted him 200 acres of land in what is now Princeton, "southeasterly from Wachusett Mountain." He sold that land later to Benjamin Houghton for 100 pounds.

He finally died, very old, in 1769, one of the last witnesses of Rutland's days of terror.

Worcester Telegram & Gazette

Mount Wachusett as it looked a generation ago, with the summit house visible for miles in all directions. No one knows where the Keyes property was located.

14

Chapter 4

The Lost Child of Mount Wachusett

THE NAME OF LUCY KEYES rings only a faint bell in the collective memory of Worcester County. Even in Princeton and Sterling few know the story of the little girl.

But 200 years ago, the whole region was haunted by a mystery that became a legend. In the evenings, around their hearth fires, farm folk who lived in Princeton and neighboring towns often told the story of Lucy Keyes and speculated about what had happened to the little girl that day on the wooded slopes of Mount Wachusett. To this day, no one knows for sure. Some think the mystery was explained by the guilty confession of a dying man 50 years after the event. Others say there was no confession.

In May 1751, Robert Keyes, his wife and three daughters moved from Shrewsbury to the eastern slope of Wachusett, where he had bought 200 acres of land. Gradually he cleared the stubborn land and built a log hut.

On April 14, 1755, Patty and Anna, aged 9 and 7, were sent by their mother to Wachusett Pond, a mile through the woods. Lucy, only 4, was told to stay home. She was playing outside when her mother went into the house. Her family never saw Lucy again.

Robert's wife called him in from the fields and they immediately began a search. The other two girls returned from their walk to the pond. They had not seen Lucy. After fruitlessly combing the immediate area and calling Lucy's name to the unanswering forest, Keyes saddled his horse and rode frantically to the nearest neighbors, four miles away.

The word spread throughout the sparsely settled region and by the next day volunteer searchers assembled from as far as 20 miles away. For days, dozens of men, women and youths tramped through the woods round about. Finally, the searchers ringed the mountain at the base and climbed slowly to the top, keeping contact by continuous shouting. But there was no answering cry from Lucy. At night, the searchers slept in the open and listened to the howls of wolves. Wolves were much on the minds of people in those days and certainly much on the mind

15

of Robert Keyes. But no torn clothes, no signs of violence or struggle were found.

Wachusett Pond was dragged to no avail. Gradually, the searchers gave up and drifted away. Hope flickered. Lucy's mother, consumed with feelings of guilt and grief, gradually became deranged. For years, it is said, she would wander down the path to the pond, calling Lucy's name and entreating the little girl to "come home to supper." Her piteous cries, heard by the neighbors, became a legend in themselves. Those who saw and heard the demented woman never forgot it.

Robert Keyes did not lose his sanity, but Lucy became an obsession. He became convinced that she had been captured by the Indians and spirited away to Canada. That is a possibility. Although there were no tribes living near Mount Wachusett in 1755, Indians were sometimes seen passing along the mountain trails.

Keyes began to track down every rumor he heard and every theory he could conjure up. When he heard that a white child was living with Indians in New Hampshire, he made the long trip only to find that the rumor originated in Canada. He sent letters and advertised in the papers, but with no results.

Years later, impoverished and weary, Keyes wrote to the General Court in Boston, praying for some relief for the expenses he had incurred looking for his lost daughter. The petition (written in the third person) still seems poignant: "The cost he hath been put to in Searching for said Child being about 100 pounds lawful money, that he is not able to bear it being in a new plantation . . ." But his petition for another tract of land in Princeton was turned down for unknown reasons.

Keyes died in 1795, a few years after his wife. Gradually, the memory of the little girl and the distraught parents faded. But generations later a startling story, told at third hand, revived the legend.

In 1859, Princeton celebrated its centennial and imported Professor Erastus Everett, of Brooklyn, N.Y., to speak. He made a casual mention of the Lucy Keyes story during his oration.

Somehow, an old lady then living in Kansas heard about it and wrote a letter to Everett. She had lived in Princeton as a girl, she said, and remembered hearing about a deathbed confession of a man named Littlejohn, who had been a neighbor of the Keyes a century before. According to the story, Littlejohn, furious at Keyes for some reason, met little Lucy in the woods and struck her on the head with a heavy stick. Fearing that his soul would roast in hell, the dying man told this tale to a minister in the hope of absolution.

In "Picturesque Worcester," published in 1895, William T. Harlow gave a graphic account of old John Littlejohn, lying on his deathbed in Deerfield, N.Y., "apparently dying for many days, suffering untold agonies of body and horrors of mind. Day after day he languishes, and languishing, doth live, longing, praying, hoping to die."

But he cannot die until he has confessed to the dreadful deed.

According to the story, Littlejohn said he had joined the search party on the first day, but managed to keep the others away from the hollow tree where he had hidden the body. In the darkness, he buried the body under a stump and then lit a fire to destroy the evidence.

As the old lady remembered the story, Littlejohn was cursed for the rest of his life with a gnawing feeling of guilt. Every time he walked through the woods, he seemed to see the little girl running before him. For years afterward, he could hear in his mind the grief-stricken calls of the distraught mother looking for her lost child.

It was a dramatic tale, but was it true? Francis Everett Blake, the official historian of Princeton, spent months studying the case. He found discrepancy after discrepancy. Littlejohn, the alleged murderer, did not live in Princeton in 1755, although he did some time later. Littlejohn never moved to Deerfield, N.Y., where the confession was supposed to have taken place. There were other inconsistencies in the story. Blake decided that the Littlejohn story did not unravel the Lucy Keyes mystery, although he was at a loss as to how the story got started.

If Mount Wachusett could talk, perhaps it could tell what happened to Lucy Keyes. But the mountain remains silent, as it has for more than two centuries.

Worcester Telegram & Gazette

Court sessions in Worcester were held in the meeting house until the first county courthouse was built in 1732 on Court Hill. A larger one was built in 1751 and served until 1802, when it was moved to Trumbull Square.

18

Chapter 5

'Whipt On Ye Naked Body Twenty Stripes'

THE WORCESTER OF 250 YEARS AGO did not believe in coddling criminals. Probation, parole and rehabilitation were far in the future. A look at the old court records shows a justice system that was swift, crude and probably effective.

Worcester was designated county seat in 1731. It was a great honor, much coveted by Oxford, Rutland, Lancaster and Brookfield. But it required the town to provide space for the Court of General Sessions of the Peace, the Inferior Court of Common Pleas, the Superior Court of Judicature, the Court of Assize and the Superior Court.

The first court sessions were held in the old meetinghouse until the splendid new courthouse, 26 by 36 feet, was opened on Court Hill, not far from where the courthouse stands now. The first jail was William Jenison's house, "by his consent." On Sept. 22, 1731, the court ordered that "a Sutable Cage be built in ye back part (of Jenison's house) and that the prison yard Shall Extend Twenty feet on the South Side and East End thereof and so far on the North Side and West end thereof as shall include ye House & Office."

A regular jail was built shortly after. In 1736, the authorities decided to upgrade the sanitary facilities. "The Court now order that a Sutable Vault for Receiving the ordure of those who are or may be Confined in the Goal (jail) in Worcester be made as soon as may be & that due care be had in making the Same Strong and well plateing the hole to be Cut through the floor into the Same & making of it very secure . . ." In other words, no embarrassing escapes.

What sorts of things did the court take up 250 years ago in Worcester? Fornication, non-attendance at church, robbery, non-support of relatives, drunkenness, that's what.

An astonishing amount of fornication seems to have gone on, considering the sparse population of the period. Men and women, singly and severally. Sometimes husbands, sometimes wives, sometimes husbands and wives. The researcher scratches his head to figure out what was going on.

19

"Nath Bartlett of Brookfield Confest himself Guilty of ye Crime of Fornication was Sentenced to pay a fine of thirty Shillings & Cost which he pd and was Dismissed." No problem there.

The same with: *"Meriam Jones wife of Daniel Jones of Brookfield Came into Court & Confessed that She was Guilty of ye Crime of Fornication was fin'd thirty Shillings and dismissed paying costs."* There are dozens like that.

But how about this one? *"Ephraim Smith of Shrewsbury & Hari his wife both being presented by ye Grandjurors for being Guilty of ye Crime of Fornication came into Court and Confessed them Selves Severally Guilty were find Each to ye King thirty Shillings & to pay Cost which they paid & were dismissed."*

There are dozens like that, too. Were those couples guilty of having a child too soon after wedlock, or was something else involved? The records give no clue.

Next to fornication, the most common offense was failing to attend church and for "Rideing Unecessaryly on ye Lords day." In those days, the church and the meetinghouse were one and the same. Separation of church and state was 150 years in the future, and would have seemed a bizarre concept, not to say against God's law, to the people of Worcester County in 1735.

"Jonathan Harwood of Sutton in ye County of Worcester husbandman appeared in Court To answer To his presentment for not attending on ye Publick Worship of God, and made his Excuse and was dismissed paying cost."

Jonathan's excuse apparently was better than the one given by Mathew Barber of Shrewsbury who *"Confessed he was Guilty of Rideing from Shrewsbury to Worcester . . . but Justifyed his So doing because his Rideing was Only from his own House To a place of Publick Worship in Worcester where he found by Experience Twas most for his Spirtuall advantage to attend."*

Good try, Mathew, but sorry. Thirty shillings fine, fifteen to go for the relief of the poor of Shrewsbury.

Besides fornicating and staying away from church, our ancestors also got drunk, stole objects that were not theirs and made themselves unwelcome in the neighborhood. It was common for town selectmen to get a court warrant to tell some undesirable person to get out of town and stay out. At just one sitting of the court in 1736, Ebenezer Slinglee and his family were told to depart Lunenburg, Martha Mackintyre was given her walking papers by Dudley, Mary Wilson by Mendon and Thomas Foster by Shrewsbury. What had these people done? Again, no clues, but town authorities in those days did not want people around who might become public charges. Chronic drunks, for example.

Drunkenness was a serious problem. In 1736, Solomon Johnson of Leicester was convicted of drunkenness and given a choice: A fine of 10 shillings or 24 hours in jail. Johnson apparently didn't have the cash, so he was committed. By that time, the town had a new prison, an oak-timbered cell 18 feet square with a stone dungeon underneath.

There were also the stocks and the pillory. And there was also the rawhide whip, as John Fitz Gerald, alias John Hayes, alias John McNeal found out in 1734. Fitz Gerald was a bad one. He had stolen 50 pounds and six silk handkerchiefs from Samuel Lawdy of Medfield even while he was being arraigned in Suffolk Court on another charge *"...all of which is highly Criminall and against ye peace of our Said Lord the King His Crown & Dignity and ye Good and whilesom Laws of this province."* Fitz Gerald pleaded not guilty and asked for a jury trial, which proved to be a mistake. The jury found him guilty, whereupon the court decreed *"...that the Said John Fitz Gerald al. John Hays Al. John M'Neal be whipt on ye naked body Twenty stripes That he pay the Said Samuel Lawdy threeble ye mony & goods stole viz one hundred & fifty nine pounds The mony and goods found To be part thereof, and upn his neglecting to pay ye Same That he be bound to ye Sd Sam Lawdy his heirs and assigns At Ten pounds per year to pay ye Saame that he pay Cost & fees taxed at fourteen pounds nine Shillings & Six pence and Stand Comitted till Sentence be performed."*

The stocks and pillory were not used much, judging by "Carl's Tour of Main Street," a series of articles that ran in the Worcester Palladium in 1855. They purported to be reminiscences of "Carl's" father about the old days:

"My father told me afterwards that he never saw but one pillory; and then a man and a woman were punished by standing in one hour, to answer the sentence of the court."

He had seen a man whipped for being a horse thief: "The cat consisted of a whip handle about a foot and a half in length, with nine small knotted cords, of about the same length. My father said that the blood spurted out of the poor fellow's back, at the first blow, wherever the knots hit him. He shrieked out at evry blow ... when the fifteen lashes had been given, the blood ran freely down the culprit's back, which looked as red as raw beef; and they then rubbed it over with soft soap, and led him back to prison."

He also saw a thief taken from jail, " ... laid upon his back in a rough box; his hands and feet secured; and the letter T pricked into his forehead with indelible ink." We may find it hard to believe that such a thing could be done in Worcester, but 'Carl' wasn't making the story up.

In 1737, Worcester had its first execution — High Hindman alias John Hamilton, for burglary.

In 1768, Arthur "a negro" was executed for rape.

In 1770, William Lindsay, for burglary.

In 1778 came the famous Bathsheba Spooner case. Bathsheba, her lover and two other British soldiers were hanged on a gallows erected east of what is now Summer Street while 5,000 people watched. Executions remained public until the next century.

It was a law and order society that our ancestors ran in those days. Guilt and innocence were clear-cut concepts. A person found guilty was punished without undue delay. There were few appeals in those days and none of the rationalizations that modern penology has devised.

Ours is a far more humane society. We would never countenance flogging, public humiliation, disfigurement and banishment from a community. We would be appalled at executing someone for burglary.

But when it comes to raw justice — for victims as well as offenders — is our system really that much better?

Worcester Telegram & Gazette

In 1900, Maria Louisa Trumbull moved the former second courthouse from Trumbull Square to Massachusetts Avenue, where it stands today as a private residence.

22

Chapter 6

Getting Across the Lake

*I*SAIAH THOMAS WAS ONE of the first to promote a direct road to Boston. He thought it a waste of time and energy to drive a horse and buggy north up Lincoln Street and around through Shrewsbury on the way to the old Post Road to Boston.

In 1804, he laid out the route — close to what is now Route 9. He organized the Worcester and Boston Turnpike Corporation to build the road. There was one major problem: Lake Quinsigamond.

There it sat, 500 feet of open water, 50 to 70 feet deep. Thomas and his colleagues stood on the steep bank and gazed across to the Shrewsbury side. How to span it? It was beyond the engineering technology and resources of the time. But someone came up with an idea — a floating bridge.

A floating bridge it was, made of a double layer of logs fastened at right angles to each other and covered with a floor of rough planks. It cost $9,000 and opened in 1807.

Hundreds of teams and thousands of people crossed that crude contraption and its successors in the next 53 years. Sometimes it was a wet experience. Many years later, the Worcester Spy reminisced about the old floating bridge:

"The approaches would be considered atrocious nowadays. They were precipitous as possible for the safety of vehicles and the buggies and carriages and wagons of those days were not so light as the present generation is accustomed to .

"The floating bridge sat low upon the water. When the waves were high . . . wheels were submerged almost hub deep; and when the powder wagons on their way from the powder mills in Barre, then a principal supply for the arsenal at Watertown and the navy yard at Charlestown, passed over, the bridge sank below the smooth-water level. The roadbed was wide enough for teams to pass."

In other words, usable but not perfection. About 10 years later, engineering skills having advanced, plans were laid for a much more elaborate bridge, one suspended several feet above the water instead of partly submerged.

Nine large structures, each measuring 30 by 30 feet, were built out of planks and beams assembled on the water, course by course. They were to be the piers

23

After years of putting up with unreliable floating bridges, Worcester in 1868 finally decided to build a causeway across Lake Quinsagamond. Thousands of yards of fill were dumped in from both sides until the gap could be spanned by the short bridge shown above. This view is to the east, toward Shrewsbury. The causeway, considered ugly by many, was finally removed and replaced by a modern bridge in 1919.

24

that supported the bridge. As each course was added, the ones below sank under the increased weight, until the first course of timbers rested on the bottom. As one account has it, "stringers were then placed on the piers, connecting them; a covering of heavy planking was laid on the stringers and a bed of gravel completed the construction."

But the engineers underestimated the treacherous, muddy bottom of Lake Quinsigamond. As people and horses and wagons began to use the bridge, the piers settled at different levels. Joints opened and timbers started from their fastenings. On Sept. 19, 1817, the still-buoyant piers floated upward, leaned, tipped and collapsed, spreading 54,000 feet of lumber on the lake.

The following winter, when the lake was frozen solid, another floating bridge was built on the ice along the west shore of the lake. In the spring, it was laboriously towed across and fastened securely at both ends. It and its successors served, with time out for repairs and maintenance, until 1841, when the Worcester Turnpike Corporation dissolved itself and turned responsibility for the lake bridge over to the city of Worcester.

The city made do with the floating bridge until the Civil War, when Mayor Isaac Davis came up with a plan — a causeway across the lake from both sides, with a short bridge in the middle. And it was done, with the help of crowds of unemployed men who had been hanging around, getting into trouble. Hundreds of tons of rock and gravel were dumped into the lake. By 1863, people for the first time could drive across Lake Quinsigamond without getting their horses' feet wet. About the turn of the century, it was widened to accommodate trolley tracks.

But the causeway was an eyesore and 'an abomination to people with valuable property around the lake. For one thing, it split the lake in two and made full-fledged rowing regattas impossible. By the 1890s, people were convinced that the causeway had to go.

In 1916, after years of political maneuvering, Mayor George M. Wright finally was able to get work started on an elegant new bridge, supported by arches broad enough and high enough to accommodate regattas and all manner of boats. The ugly causeway was removed. On July 31, 1919, a full year after the specified completion date, the new bridge opened in a spectacular gala, with 25,000 on hand joining in the festivities.

That bridge lasted for 64 years, when the state rebuilt it and widened it to four lanes. If old Isaiah Thomas were around to visit Spag's, he surely would approve.

The Worcester Bank, left, was opened for business on May 8, 1805. It served as the bank and as the residence for Daniel Waldo Jr. until 1830, when he moved into his new mansion, right. The bank building burned down in 1843. The Waldo mansion was moved in 1855 to make way for the new Mechanics Hall. For many years, it was an inn.

DANIEL WALDO JR.

26

Chapter 7

The First Worcester-Boston Bank War

WHEN THE SHAWMUT BANK of Boston bought Worcester County National Bank in 1983, that rumbling sound from Rural Cemetery must have been Daniel Waldo Jr. gnashing his teeth. Waldo, president of the Worcester Bank for 41 years, fought many a stout battle to keep the Boston bankers' noses out of the Worcester banking picture.

The most notable confrontation came on July 26, 1826, when a man from the Suffolk Bank walked up to the Worcester Bank counter, presented two packages of bills issued by the Worcester Bank and demanded immediate payment in gold or silver specie. The bills added up to more than $48,000 — more than half the entire amount that the bank had outstanding. Waldo understood what was at stake; the Suffolk was threatening to break the Worcester Bank in order to get concessions that would enable it to dominate banking in Massachusetts. It was not his first joust with the Suffolk.

Waldo took the man into his office and tried to reach an understanding. He gave the Suffolk messenger $28,000 in specie and said that the balance would be available the following day at the New England Bank in Boston, where the Worcester Bank had $39,000 in credits. He would make out a draft for the balance, which would be honored at the New England Bank.

The Suffolk man took the specie, according to agreement, but he said that the draft would be accepted under only one condition: that the Worcester Bank agree to use the Suffolk Bank as its Boston depositary. Waldo refused. The next day he sent William Jennison, cashier, to Boston to pay off the $20,000. The Suffolk Bank refused to accept it. Suffolk officials said they would accept payment in specie only at the counter of the Worcester Bank, as previously agreed — unless, of course, the Worcester Bank agreed to deposit its funds at the Suffolk Bank. Jennison said no. The Suffolk then made its next move, which obviously had been carefully planned.

In the words of the outraged Worcester Bank directors, "What then was our astonishment, at three o'clock the next day, to be addressed by a Sheriff, charged with a special writ of attachment to secure upon the real estate the Corporation, the above mentioned balance of $20,000, upon a writ, too, made in Boston at the instance of the directors of the Suffolk Bank, after an interview with them by our Cashier, with the money in his possession to satisfy the claims and forwarded by an express through the country, at the rate of ten miles an hour, to attach real estate, in the security for the payment of bank bills, for which the specie was offered before the process was issued."

That makes the Suffolk Bank sound like a grasping villain. Actually, it was motivated by more than greed. Suffolk was trying to introduce order into the state's chaotic banking system. In those days, every bank issued its own bills, payable on demand. The bills were used instead of specie, which was always scarce. When the bills were presented at the banks that had issued them, they were redeemed at full value. But when they were redeemed at other banks, they were often discounted. Boston banks regularly discounted the bills of the various "country banks," which the country bankers resented exceedingly. As far as Boston was concerned, the Worcester Bank was just another small-town bank run by small-town people.

That attitude may partly explain the stubborn reaction of Waldo and the Worcester Bank trustees. At this late date, there is no way to find out what was on their minds or why they favored the New England Bank over the Suffolk Bank. But there is no question that they saw the Suffolk's plans as a threat to their independence that had to be rebuffed.

The Worcester Bank had been organized in 1804, the first bank in the state west of Boston. People today may find it astonishing that the town had got along without any bank for almost 100 years. As the county seat and something of a trading and mechandising center, Worcester needed cash and credit and a reliable system to provide them. Without a bank, how in the world did a man get the money to start in trade or business or to buy a house or a horse?

The answer is: He borrowed the money from one of the people who loaned money, most likely Daniel Waldo Jr. or Stephen Salisbury.

For example, in Feb. 28, 1803, one Amasa Southwick of Leicester, who wanted to expand his cardmaking business, signed a note to Waldo promising to pay "him or his Order, the value of Four hundred and Nine spanish milled Dollars and Fifty eight cents in Gold or Silver, on Demand, with lawful Interest, in like Money."

It was a simple system, and it worked fairly well. By 1804, however, the influential citizens of Worcester — men like Stephen Salisbury, Isaiah Thomas, Daniel Waldo Sr., Daniel Waldo Jr., Samuel Flagg, William Paine, Nathan Patch, Francis Blake — decided that the community needed a bank to put lending and record keeping on a more regular basis. At a meeting at Barker's Tavern in December 1803, they decided to ask Worcester residents to buy shares in a new "country bank." Three weeks later they petitioned the Massachusetts Legislature for a bank capitalized at $150,000. The 1,500 shares offered at $100 apiece were all sold by March 1 and the bank was chartered on March 8, 1804.

Then began the long struggle with the Boston banks, particularly the Suffolk Bank. For a time, from 1807 to 1810, the Worcester Bank issued "facilities" in an attempt to stop the ruinous discounting of Worcester Bank notes in Boston. Facilities were not promissory notes, but an actual substitute for money, widely used as such. Traders took them in payment for their goods, for they could be redeemed at full value at the Worcester Bank and other banks at any time.

Nonetheless, the Suffolk Plan continued to spread. The Worcester Bank was one of the main holdouts. The Suffolk found this insubordination intolerable.

When the Suffolk decided to bring the Worcester Bank to heel in 1826, it made careful plans. Apparently it collected Worcester Bank bills and squirreled them away until it knew it had accumulated an amount too large for the Worcester Bank to redeem in specie all at once. Then it sent its agent, bills in hand, to Worcester for the confrontation. From the Boston point of view, Worcester would have no choice but to agree to deposit funds in the Suffolk Bank. But things didn't turn out that way, thanks to the determination (or stubbornness) of Daniel Waldo Jr. and his friends.

When the Suffolk Bank refused the specie payment from cashier Samuel Jennison on that July day, he deposited the $20,000 in the New England Bank to the credit of the Suffolk Bank and notified the Suffolk Bank that the money was there for the asking.

The Suffolk didn't back down. It went to court, claiming damages of 24 percent a year on the $20,000, on the theory that the Worcester Bank had refused to pay a lawful obligation. But in March 1827, the court ruled that the Worcester Bank had acted in good faith.

Thus was born an enduring suspicion in Worcester of Boston banks and Boston's motives. The Worcester Bank stayed out of the Suffolk system as long as Waldo lived and even after. Not until 30 years later did the directors of the Worcester Bank vote "that accounts be opened with the Suffolk Bank for the redemption of our bills."

And not until almost 160 years later did a Boston bank succeed in buying out the descendant of the proud Worcester Bank, lock, stock and barrel. Daniel Waldo Jr. had been long since forgotten. Times change.

29

Joseph Palmer's gravestone in Leominster.

Chapter 8

"Old Jew Palmer," Defender of Freedom

SOME TIME IN 1830, the Worcester County Jail on Summer Street received a prisoner from Fitchburg named Joseph Palmer. Before he was released a year later — against his will — he had become a national celebrity and a symbol of individual conscience standing firm in the face of social intolerance.

Palmer was the victim of one of the strangest persecutions in American history. He was attacked, reviled, shunned, spit on and jailed because he insisted on his right to wear a beard.

It was a glorious beard — full flowing and patriarchal. Palmer looked much the way Walt Whitman would look 40 years later. He looked like an Old Testament prophet. He looked like Moses coming down from Mount Sinai. But he didn't look like anybody else in America except for a few Orthodox Jews. American Christians 150 years ago weren't supposed to look like Jews. When he walked along the streets of Fitchburg, the boys followed him jeering, "Old Jew Palmer."

It all seems strange to latter-day Americans, who are familiar with the pictures of Abraham Lincoln, Rutherford B. Hayes, Ulysses B. Grant, James B. Garfield and other American worthies who sported full beards. But that was later. Lincoln was the first U.S. president to wear a beard, and he grew it only after he was elected. Until 1860, American men, with few exceptions, were clean-shaven.

As Stewart Holbrook has pointed out, most of the Pilgrims and Puritans wore beards. But as time passed, beards and mustaches got smaller and smaller. By 1720, the colonists were all clean-shaven, as shown by the portraits done by John Singleton Copley, Gilbert Stuart and Ralph Earle. Washington and his generals were all beardless. Not a single signer of the Declaration of Independence had as much as a whisker.

It's not clear just why facial hair went out of fashion after 1720 and it's not clear why Joseph Palmer decided to grow a beard in 1830. Once, when he was asked that question for the umpteenth time, he said he wished that someone could explain to him why men daily wanted to scrape their faces with a steel blade

31

from the nose to the neck. But that probably wasn't the real reason; Palmer was a man of conviction, and once he had reached a conviction, nothing in heaven and earth could shake him.

When Palmer settled in Fitchburg in 1830, people couldn't believe their eyes. Although he was honest and industrious, and although he went to church every Sunday, he was plagued and tormented by the people of the town. The boys taunted him everywhere he went. People approaching him on the street would cross to the other side. His own pastor, the Rev. George Trask, reproached him. But Palmer had an answer for the minister; Jesus was always represented with a full beard. Also, the Bible has many references to beards, none pejorative. Palmer knew every scriptural quotation relating to facial hair.

Nonetheless, it was in church, at Sunday morning service, where he got into trouble. It was communion Sunday. When Palmer, with the rest, knelt for the bread and wine, the officiating clergyman ignored him. To the amazement and scandal of the congregation, Palmer strode to the communion table, drank from the cup and shouted, "I love my Jesus as well, and better, than any of you!"

A day or two later, as he was coming out of the Fitchburg Hotel, Palmer was seized by four men armed with shears, soap, brush and a razor who said that his beard was going to be shaved, then and there. In the scuffle, Palmer pulled out a

Worcester Telegram & Gazette

The old Worcester County Jail on Summer Street, where Joseph Palmer became a celebrity.

32

jackknife and stabbed two of his assailants in the legs. He saved his beard, but was soon charged "with an unprovoked assault." He refused to pay the fine and was committed to the jail in Worcester, where he stayed for more than a year.

By the end of that time, he had become a cause celebre. His letters to the Worcester Spy had won him sympathy, if not understanding. People read the stories about how other prisoners, egged on by the guards, attacked him and tried to clip his beard. They read about how he was put into solitary confinement for weeks at a time. They began to ask about the Constitution and why it said nothing about wearing beards.

Eventually, after more than a year of rising criticism, the sheriff came to Palmer and said the fine would be forgiven if Palmer would just agree to leave. No dice, said Palmer. It was a matter of principle. By that time he may have been enjoying his notoriety as the bearded prisoner of Worcester.

In the end, they had to carry him out to the sidewalk in a chair and leave him there. He still had his beard.

There is more to the Joseph Palmer story. When Bronson Alcott and others announced that they were setting up a communal farm named Fruitlands in Harvard, Palmer was one of the first to sign on. Fruitlands was an economic flop. The talkative theorists who presided there had no concept of what was required to make a farm produce. But Palmer did. He brought his own horse and plow to till the soil and kept the colony from starving. When the Transcendentalists moved on, he bought the farm and lived there for more than 20 years, running his own peculiar kind of communal enterprise.

In later life, when beards were as common as bonnets, Palmer became something of a counterculture folk hero. Once, in Fitchburg, he met the same Rev. Trask who years before had scolded the Palmer beard. Rev. Trask by then sported a beard. Palmer could not resist stroking his own beard and saying, "Knowest thou that thy redeemer liveth?"

Palmer is buried in a North Leominster cemetery. On his monument is a stone carving of him as he must have looked, his noble beard rampant and flowing. The caption is apt: "Persecuted for Wearing the Beard."

Let's remember "Old Jew Palmer." He was not Jewish, but he struck a blow for individual freedom and the right to be different. Any society can use people like that.

33

Worcester Historical Museum

The canal fever of the 1820s and 1830s died away when the railroads began chugging across the land. In 1848, the last barge used the Blackstone Canal. After that, the canal — smelly, fetid, crumbling — fell into decay. In the 1890s, the city of Worcester began to enclose the canal, which it used as its main sewer. The aqueduct shown above was not enough to protect the Centrum from the floods of 1982 and 1985. A much bigger aqueduct was being pushed to completion in late 1985.

34

Chapter 9

Take the Next Boat to Ashburnham

MOST PEOPLE IN WORCESTER COUNTY know the story of the Blackstone Canal, chartered by Massachusetts and Rhode Island in 1823 and opened for business in 1828.

But how many have heard about the canal linking Boston and Springfield via Worcester? Or the one via Fitchburg, Ashburnham and Gardner? How many have heard of the canal from Springfield to Albany, including the 20-foot-wide tunnel through the Hoosac Range? What about the canal along the Charles River to connect South Boston to Milford and "thence to the Blackstone" where it would link up with the Blackstone Canal, just then getting underway?

Well, those canals were not built. They were only proposed. But they had fervent boosters. Engineers endorsed them. In 1826, the Massachusetts Legislature commissioned a study of the best routes between Boston and Albany. Had it not been for the arrival of the railroad, Springfield shippers might one day have sent their goods to Boston by barge through Athol and Fitchburg.

The early part of the century was a time of canal fever in New England and the country in general. The Middlesex Canal, begun in 1794, finally linked the Merrimack and Charles Rivers in 1803. The 55-mile New Haven and Northhampton Canal along the Connecticut River was completed in 1835. In the 1820s, visionaries dreamed of a canal across Cape Cod, connecting Barnstable and Buzzards Bays. That canal was built — 90 years later. There were others in that era.

But it was the Erie Canal, between Albany and Buffalo, that caught the imagination of the American people when the first barges traversed it in 1825. It opened up the West with an all-water route to New York City and was a sensational success. "Clinton's Ditch," which had cost $7 million to build, took in $8.5 million in tolls in its first nine years. Once it was opened, freight costs from Buffalo to New York City dropped from $100 to $15 a ton, and the time from 20 days to eight.

All during the years that the Erie Canal was being built, Boston shipping interests realized what was at stake. With direct water connections to Buffalo,

35

Lake Erie and the West, New York would soon become the commercial capital of the nation. How could Boston tap into that huge stream of trade? As the visionaries of the time saw it, a canal from Boston to Albany would divert the shipping eastward across Massachusetts. Boston, not New York, would become the trade nexus of America. Bankers, businessmen, tradesmen, shipowners and speculators dreamed these heady dreams 160 years ago.

On March 1, 1825, Elias Haskell Derby wrote an open letter to Mayor Josiah Quincy of Boston urging his support for a Boston-Albany canal. Derby, who said he had studied the great canals of Europe, gave his opinion that the route should swing north of Worcester through Waltham, Weston, Sudbury, Stow and Lancaster, or else through Cambridge, Lexington, Concord, Acton, Boxboro, Harvard and Shirley, both routes arriving at the Nashua River in Fitchburg, at which point several locks would have to be built. Derby said that an "aqueduct bridge" across the Concord River might be needed, but the engineering difficulties did not seem to trouble him. One remarkable thing about those early canal planners was the blithe way they shrugged off the formidable construction problems.

West of Fitchburg, Derby favored a canal route through Gardner, Templeton and Athol, staying south of the Ashburnham ponds and linking up with the Millers River. From there, downhill to the Connecticut, across to Deerfield and up to Adams. Derby got a bit vague about the details of this part of the route, which was understandable. Not even the builders of the Erie Canal had proposed crossing a mountain range.

Worcester Historical Museum

A view of the Blackstone Canal, around 1830. The canal's Worcester terminus was near the location of the Central Fire Station.

36

Derby's letter, printed in the Massachusetts Spy and probably other newspapers, stirred up interest. Another letter writer, whose initials were "A.B.," commended Derby and suggested a few modifications. A.B. thought that the canal probably should pass through Winchendon and Ashburnham. But he suggested that the Legislature decide the matter.

It didn't take the Legislature long to get into the act. It hired Col. Loammi Baldwin, chief engineer on the Middlesex Canal and developer of the Baldwin apple, to survey the various routes. The Worcester contingent wanted a canal that went through Worcester, but Baldwin concluded that would not be feasible without the water rights to the Blackstone River and its tributaries. Those had been bought up by the Blackstone Canal Corporation, which had just started to dig its own big ditch.

Like Derby, Baldwin eventually favored the northern Worcester County route through Fitchburg, Gardner and Ashburnham. The canal, he said, should be 28 feet wide, with locks 14 feet wide and 80 feet long. He estimated the cost of construction from Boston to the Connecticut River at $3 million.

Baldwin studied the route west of the Connecticut in more detail than Derby had. He concluded that the Berkshires posed a problem. The solution he proposed was a four-mile tunnel 20 feet wide and 13 feet high through the Hoosac Range. Sixty years later, a tunnel was blasted through the mountains at about the place Baldwin had recommended. But that tunnel was for trains, not barges.

The canal proposals of that era are astonishing. A canal across Massachusetts would have to go from sea level to 1,150 feet above sea level to pass through Ashburnham. Just the section from the Connecticut River to the New York line would have required 220 locks. The canal would have required aqueduct canals, enormous cuts through hills and vast amounts of water to fill the locks as the ships passed through. The Erie Canal had bedazzled everyone. Included in the 1826 legislative report on canal routes is a letter from citizens of Rutland, Paxton, Oakham, Hardwick, New Braintree and Ware. They wanted the canal to pass through their towns, if possible.

The thought of boats and barges sailing tranquilly through the fields of Oakham and Rutland, not to mention the hills of Templeton and Winchendon, gives pause.

In the meantime, construction of the Blackstone Canal had started in 1824. Excitement was at fever pitch. When capital stock in the canal was offered to the public simultaneously in Worcester and Providence on April 27, 1825, 11,272 shares worth $1,127,900 were subscribed for in three hours. The canal was built for about $750,000 and, in October 1828, the first barge arrived in Worcester from Providence. The Blackstone Canal never paid a single dividend to its stockholders. Its best year was in 1832, when it took in $18,907 in tolls, not enough to cover costs and maintenance. It closed for good and its facilities were auctioned off in 1848, one year after the Providence and Worcester Railroad was completed. In 1897, the Worcester Telegram started a short-lived crusade to reopen the Blackstone Canal, but the idea went nowhere.

Similarly, the New Haven and Northhampton Canal never made any money for its investors, even though it carried a lot of tonnage during the few years it operated.

Railroad trains started tooting across the land in the 1830s. Except for a few outstanding exceptions like the Erie Canal, most waterways could not haul goods as cheaply and efficiently as the iron horse could. It's perhaps just as well. Who would want to go by barge through Ashburnham?

Chapter 10

Worcester and the Great Whig Conclave

WORCESTER HAS HAD SOME rousing political rallies in the last couple of centuries. But for sheer, boisterous, tub-thumping extravagance, the 1840 Whig Convention was in a class by itself.

The convention was held in a log cabin 100 feet long and 50 feet wide, specially built for the occasion on Grove Street, about where the North Works complex is now. On top was a flagpole 99 feet tall, with Old Glory waving triumphantly on top.

The parade started from the Common, which was packed with people. From there, a stately procession of full-size log cabins on huge wagons moved north along Main Street. Some were pulled by 12, some by 16, one by 22 horses. Bands played. Politicians waved to the roaring crowds. Men on horses galloped up and down.

The Worcester Spy reported that "From the Common, the procession passed through a magnificent arch, erected by the citizens of Worester and splendidly decorated with flags and streamers . . . the glorious stars and stripes were suspended from arches and trees, and festooned from windows and floated from hundreds of flagstaffs in every direction. The sashes were taken out of many of the windows fronting upon the street, and every opening and balcony upon the buildings was thronged with ladies, gaily dressed for the occasion, who cheered and encouraged their Whig friends by the waving of handkerchiefs and other significant tokens of approbation . . . which were gallantly answered by . . . the waving of hats and banners, by a flourish of trumpets and a roll of drums."

That was Worcester on June 17, 1840, the day of the Whig convention that nominated "Honest John Davis" for governor and gave boisterous acclaim to the national Whig ticket of Gen. William Henry Harrison and John Tyler.

Worcester then was a town of about 7,500. There were 10,000 delegates at the convention, according to the Massachusetts Spy, and there were thousands of spectators. We don't have political rallies in that class any more.

The 1840 contest between Harrison and President Martin Van Buren, Demo-

39

crat, was a contest of personalities and slogans. The issues, such as they were, were either buried in bombast or ignored. The main campaign theme on the Whig side was created from a Democratic slur against Harrison — that he would be happy on his backwoods Ohio farm with a pension, a log cabin and a barrel of cider. Whig strategists seized on it. Yes, why shouldn't the Whig Party be the party of log cabins and cider? That was a lot more simple than trying to make sense out of the national banking crisis. They invented a slogan — "Tippecanoe and Tyler, too." Harrison, 68, had won the Battle of Tippecanoe against the Indians years before. It was his only real claim to distinction.

Modern political strategists could take lessons from those 1840 Whig campaign managers who kept Harrison safely at home on his farm while a special committee issued platitudinous statements in his name.

The Log Cabin campaign was one of the most sensational successes in U.S. political history. Whig partisans built log cabins everywhere — and supplied them with free cider and stronger spirits.

The Worcester convention was a classic example of that campaign. Worcester County, with perhaps no more than 50,000 people, put on a show that the whole state remembered for generations. The Spy, ecstatically pro-Whig, listed some of the elements of that epic parade:

Five barouches, each drawn by four horses, carrying SOLDIERS OF THE REVOLUTION. Each carriage bore the motto: "Whigs of 1776."

JOHN DAVIS

John Davis, born in Northboro in 1787, married George Bancroft's sister, Eliza, practised law in Worcester and was elected to Congress in 1824, where he served four terms. In 1840, he was elected governor of Massachusetts in the great Whig "log cabin" campaign. From 1845 to 1853 he served in the U.S. Senate. He died in Worcester in 1854, aged 67.

40

The Sturbridge delegation, in two log cabins, capable of holding 100 persons and drawn by 22 horses.

The Hopkinton delegation, dressed as working men in white frocks trimmed with red and carrying shovels, axes and brooms, followed by a full band and a log cabin. They had walked all the way from Hopkinton.

The Ashburnham delegation, with a band on a large float, carried a sign: "THE LABORERS OF ASHBURNHAM WILL NOT WORK FOR TWENTY CENTS A DAY," a reference to the hard times caused by the collapse of the banks and the reversion to hard money.

The Leicester delegation, 200 strong, carrying banners proclaiming: "WE NEED RELIEF — WE DEMAND REFORM" and "NO REDUCTION OF WAGES."

The Marlboro delegation with a banner: "DOES HARRISON USE GOLD SPOONS? NO! WHO DOES? MARTIN VAN BUREN."

The Salem contingent had a tableau showing Harrison and Tyler, "The People's Candidates." Some of the commentary was blunt: "These are none of your dust-licking reptiles, close, insinuating, speckled, smooth Court Serpents; but Honest Men that have a troublesome way of shocking the Country's ears with horrid truths."

Library of Congress

The 1840 presidential contest was the first modern political campaign. It featured bands, rallies, free drinks, and a symbol — the log cabin, a reminder of Whig William Henry Harrison's modest beginnings as contrasted to the decadent luxury attributed to President Martin Van Buren. As the accompanying cartoon shows, the Democrats tried to ridicule the log cabin theme as a trap for the unwary, but to no avail. Harrison won handily.

41

A picture of Van Buren was labeled: "Martin Van Buren. Beneath whose outside froth, fermenting, lie Pride, Envy, Faction, Turbulence of soul, a secret Traitor, equally unfit to obey or rule."

The Sutton delegation carried a banner that brought oldtimers back to Revolutionary Days. It read:

IT'S ALL OVER
HERE COMES OLD SUTTON, AS LONG AS ETERNITY

Tory John Chandler is supposed to have uttered that line in 1775, when he saw the Sutton contingent march into Worcester to join the other militia for duty against the British.

And there were dozens more all blending in one vast political extravaganza. Worcester, Massachusetts and the country were going through a spasm of political partisanship of a sort that comes only once in most lifetimes.

What had so roused the good people of Massachusetts to such a frenzy? The main complaint was the hard times that followed the financial panic of 1837, when the value of paper money — issued by banks — collapsed.

Library of Congress

The Harrison campaign was the first to use the log cabin theme. It was used many times later, notably by Abraham Lincoln's political strategists in 1860.

42

The enemy was Van Buren, considered foppish, extravagant, untrustworthy and uncaring. By then, the Van Buren Democrats were usually castigated as "Locofocos." The Locofocos (named for the new friction matches that flared up when scratched) were the hard-money faction of the party. These hard-money Democrats were appalled by the wild currency speculation and inflation after Andrew Jackson killed the Bank of the United States. Originally a minority, their views finally prevailed. But the deflation that followed the inflation had made Van Buren intensely unpopular, especially in the East and the commercial sectors of the country. Gold and silver money were scarce. Men were working for 25 cents a day.

That emotional political spree in Worcester on June 17, 1840, was one of many all over the eastern seaboard. In November, Harrison and Tyler swept New England and most of the country. Harrison got 234 electoral votes to Van Buren's 60. Shortly after his inauguration on March 4, 1841, he caught a cold that went into his chest. He died on April 4, the first president not to complete his term.

American Antiquarian Society

William H. Harrison, winner of the Battle of Tippecanoe in 1811 and a colonel in the war of 1812, was almost 70 when he was picked by the Whigs to run for president in 1840. A brilliant public relations effort convinced the people that he was a qualified candidate.

43

Worcester Telegram & Gazette

St. John's Church, circa 1880

44

Chapter 11

When They Drove the Priest Out of Town

O N PALM SUNDAY IN 1847, a mob of angry Irishmen raged into Washington Square and invaded Donlevie's Tavern, where they finished off the liquor. They headed up Grafton Street toward a brewery, where they were turned away by a cool-headed watchman who said no liquor was stored there on weekends. They roared down Water Street, throwing bricks and smashing windows — especially windows that flaunted lace curtains. They headed up Green Street to Tobias Boland's house. Fortunately for everybody, Boland wasn't home.

Some of them continued on down Temple Street where they collared Rev. Matthew Gibson in the St. John's rectory and roughed him up. Frightened by the threatening mob, he boarded up the rectory's doors and windows and fled to Boston on the night train.

The Palm Sunday riot was one of the saddest episodes in the history of Worcester's Irish. Like a bolt of lightning in the night, it illuminated the festering rancor between the various divisions of the Irish — the West Country people vs. the East Country people, the Gaelic speakers vs. the English speakers, the laborers vs. the foremen, even the laborers who did dog work vs. the laborers who had easier, more coveted jobs.

The attack on Father Gibson was almost symbolic. He was English, not Irish, and he wore fancy clerical garb. The new immigrants were in a strange land, and everywhere they looked they saw oppressors, especially in their own church and among their own people.

As Timothy J. Meagher points out in his fine history of St. John's Parish, "To Preserve the Flame," the roots of the explosion of 1847 went back hundreds of years, back to Oliver Cromwell and even beyond. For centuries there had been two Irelands, one bleakly impoverished, the other less so.

The first Irish immigrants who arrived in Worcester came from the eastern side of the Emerald Isle. They came in the 1820s to work on the Blackstone Canal. In the 1830s, they built the Boston and Worcester Railroad, which opened on the

45

Fourth of July, 1835. They worked hard, suffered innumerable accidents and lived under primitive conditions, but they gradually forged their way upward in a suspicious society. A few of them, such as Tobias Boland, did very well. Boland was the main contractor for the Blackstone Canal, and it made him rich.

By the 1840s, the Irish immigrant stream began to include more and more people from the west of Ireland, the most poverty-stricken and backward part of the land. Those people, many of whom spoke Gaelic, looked with envy and suspicion on the earlier Irish settlers who could speak fluent English and who lived in decent tenements instead of shanties and held down the better jobs.

They particularly hated people like the wealthy Tobey Boland, whom they called "Lord Normandsby," after a notorious English landlord in Ireland who ground the faces of the Irish peasants. They saw Boland and his ilk as the hand-maidens of the ruling class. One of Boland's crimes was that he had begun hiring French Canadians on his construction jobs because they supposedly were more tractable than the new Irish. In 1845, the Irish workers had demanded that Father Gibson fire Boland as contractor for the new St. John's Church on Temple Street, and Father Gibson reluctantly acceded.

Trouble had been brewing ever since Bishop Benedict Fenwick assigned Father Gibson to Worcester. The immigrants hated him and his haughty English manner. But that was less dangerous than the growing split between the new immigrants and the established Irish people. In 1846, the secret Shamrock Society

BISHOP BENEDICT FENWICK

REV. MATTHEW GIBSON

46

began to attract the bitterest of the men, many of whom were unemployed. Tensions rose. At about that time, news of the hideous famine in Ireland began to reach Worcester. The stories from Ireland in the 1840s compare with those from Ethiopia in the 1980s. By March, 1847, the Spy was running regular dispatches from Ireland. One of its correspondents was Elihu Burritt, the famed "learned blacksmith" who had taught himself a dozen languages and lectured all over the world. His report from "this region of the shadow of death" is harrowing, even today.

Meagher thinks that the desperation in Ireland fueled the desperation of the immigrants in Worcester and gave to the Palm Sunday riot its "special frenzy." In the spring of 1847, a pitiful lot of humanity arrived in Boston from Ireland on the *Hibernia* — "tattered, half-starved, dying of ship's fever, typhus and cholera." They died by the hundreds in Boston and Worcester, many in rooms hastily readied in the new St. John's Church.

St. John's Church, dedicated on July 24, 1846, was a source of great pride, but it did not unify the various elements of Father Gibson's flock. He seemed to side with the rich and the powerful against the poor and the unruly. When he was instructed by Bishop Fitzpatrick to investigate the charges made by the Shamrock Society against the bosses and shopkeepers about exploitation, he said he found no substance in such complaints. He hated and feared the Shamrock Society and condemned it in public. But it went underground and spawned rival gangs that committed crimes and terrorized the people who lived in the largely Irish East Side.

But just when everything seemed the blackest and bleakest, some rays of hope were seen. Rev. John Boyce was assigned as co-pastor with Father Gibson, and proved popular. A group of Irish veterans from the Mexican War organized the Jackson Guards, a vigilante force that battled the gangs and criminals in Scalpintown and brought a degree of order to things.

The time of troubles bred more troubles. The influx of Irish into Worcester (3,000 in five years) stirred up the fires and rancors of nativism and anti-Catholicism. George Richardson, candidate of the Know Nothings for mayor, swept into office with 70 percent of the vote in 1854.

But even while all that was happening, other currents were running. Holy Cross College, destroyed by fire in 1852, was being rebuilt, stone by stone, mostly by Catholic efforts, but also with some help from Protestants. Richardson was succeeded as mayor by Isaac Davis, Alexander Bullock and William W. Rice, three honorable men. In a few years, the Civil War would sweep away not only slavery but also Know-Nothingism. Much of the old anti-Catholic feeling was dissipated in that national cauldron.

47

On July 28, 1884, St. John's celebrated its 50th anniversary as a parish. Three bishops were on hand along with a "host" of priests and all sorts of dignitaries. Sacred music was performed by a 13-piece orchestra and a choir selected from the five Catholic parishes in Worcester. More than 10,000 people attended the various services at St. John's. James Mellen, editor of the Worcester Daily Times, wrote that it was the "greatest event" in Worcester Catholic history.

St. John's and its people had come a long way, but there were more accomplishments on the near horizon. In 1900, 44 years after Know-Nothing Mayor Richardson left City Hall, Philip O'Connell would be elected mayor of Worcester, the first Irish Catholic to hold that post.

Thus, although the Palm Sunday riot in Worcester and the ghastly famine in Ireland marked a terrible time of troubles, it was not the end. Even then, there were glimmerings of light on the dark horizon.

Chapter 12

Worcester — Birthplace of Women's Rights

IN 1983, PLANNED PARENTHOOD of Central Massachusetts opened a clinic at 340 Main St., Worcester, to help women with problems relating to pregnancy.

That location is a historic spot for women. It was there, in old Brinley Hall, that the movement for women's rights achieved a national forum 133 years earlier.

The organized women's rights movement in this country began at a meeting at Seneca Falls, N.Y., in 1848. A second women's convention was held in Rochester, N.Y., in 1849. But the National Woman's Rights Convention held in Worcester on Oct. 23 and 24, 1850, was the first that captured national attention and support. That, and the second Woman's Rights Convention held in Worcester one year later, made the feminist movement a national issue.

The 1850 convention ran into fierce opposition from some. One account ridiculed it as "a motley gathering of fanatical mongrels, of old grannies, male and female, of fugitive slaves and fugitive lunatics." James Gordon Bennett's New York Herald called it an "awful combination of Socialism, Abolitionism and Infidelity" and reported the "gloomy and warlike" appearance of the delegates. The Herald noted that there was not one baby in evidence and "not a whisper, or an insinuation, that babies are necessary to the preservation of society . . ." It predicted that the Woman's Rights Convention was destined "to stumble over the cradle." That argument would be heard again and again over the generations.

But the convention was much more than "fanatical mongrels." It attracted more than 1,000 delegates from 11 states, including some of the most distinguished intellects in the land. It was called to order by Sarah H. Earle, wife of the editor and publisher of the Worcester Spy, John Milton Earle. Among the speakers were Lucretia Mott, Lucy Stone, Abby Kelley Foster, Paulina Wright Davis, Wendell Phillips, William Lloyd Garrison, William Henry Channing and Stephen S. Foster, husband of Abby.

The Spy, not surprisingly, was impressed: "We have known no convention or other public meeting held in this city where all the exercises were conducted

49

with more decorum or in better spirit, or where the whole of the speaking has been more uniformly able and unobjectionable. We . . . had not looked for such a display of forensic talent as we witnessed in the female speakers especially."

That undoubtedly was true. Abby Kelley Foster had years of experience on the lecture circuit. She was noted for her ability to rivet her audiences with her fiery denunciations. Lucretia Mott and Paulina Davis were experienced speakers. A dazzling performance was given by Lucy Stone, one of the finest public speakers, male or female, that this country has ever produced, judging by contemporary accounts. Her power came not only from her command of her subject and the force of her convictions, but from a compellingly beautiful voice, much remarked on by persons who heard her speak.

Another who made a strong impression on the Spy reporter was "Mrs. Rose of New York, who we learn, was by birth a Polish Jewess." That was Ernestine Rose, born Siismund Potoski, daughter of a rabbi, married to an Englishman and one of the famous reformers of the time. Alice Felt Tyler, author of "Freedom's Ferment," describes Mrs. Rose in glowing terms: "Handsome and cultivated, an able speaker with great dignity and quick wit, she became one of the most valuable of the suffragist lecturers, speaking often and before large audiences in every northern state."

There was one professional woman on the platform — Harriet K. Hunt of Boston, a physician. She made an "especially telling" address on the importance of women becoming doctors. "We ask for no separate medical colleges, we ask for no apppropriation of public money; but we do ask — in the fear of the Lord — in the trust that our claim is right and proper . . . we do ask for women EQUAL medical advantages with those enjoyed by men." Dr. Hunt would live to see women accepted at medical schools and become surgeons as well as general practitioners.

H.H. Van Amringe dealt with a perennial issue in the women's rights debate — the bearing of arms. "If the employments of priests, teachers, physicians and judges are causes of exen.ption from military service, then this objection, in regard to women, is utterly insignificant."

Abby A. Price said that the issue was chiefly economic. She argued for "equal opportunities with men for suitable and *well compensated* employment . . . "When she is engaged in the same occupation with men, her remuneration is greatly below what is awarded to her stronger associates."

The speeches and discussions in Brinley Hall have a contemporary ring. The delegates pointed out that the Declaration of Independence phrase, "all men are created equal," left out half the human race. There were many references to the "bondage" — legal and social — that women labored under. Wendell Phillips

LUCY STONE JULIA WARD HOWE

PAULINA W. DAVIS ABBY KELLEY FOSTER

There were many brilliant women in the feminist movement of the last century. The four pictured here were among the most outstanding.

Library of Congress Photos

51

skewered the injustice of Massachusetts law with an account of a moderately wealthy Massachusetts woman who married a man without means. Under the law, her property became her husband's. He died after a year or so of marriage, leaving her the money that had been hers before she married, with one provision: She would forfeit it if she married again.

A major issue then, and for many years after, was women's suffrage. Speaker after speaker scoffed at the sexist assumption that women were incapable of casting an intelligent ballot, while "every barroom brawler" was given that high responsibility.

Yet some were not convinced. Although progressive newspapers like the Spy and Horace Greeley's New York Tribune praised the convention, Bennett's New York Herald, and other Boston and New York papers, did not. The Worcester Palladium, an anti-Abolitionist, anti-reform organ, ridiculed the whole idea: "The women who figured in this convention seemed to have no thought beyond the idea of giving political rights to their sex, in order that they might become voters, public speakers, representatives, senators, governors, presidents, preachers, lawyers, etc. Now the women if they are going to make men of themselves should make up their minds to take the burdens as well as the honors of men ..."

It may have been more than a coincidence that the convention was held in Worcester. Central Massachusetts had reared some of the nation's outstanding feminists, both men and women.

There were Abby Kelley Foster and Stephen S. Foster, a remarkable couple dedicated to ridding society of all kinds of oppression. They were crusaders for Abolition, for women's rights, for women's suffrage, for total equality between man and woman. On Dec. 21, 1845, they married themselves in a simple ceremony and signed a contract in which they stated that they had "consummated a matrimonial connection ... by a public display of our mutual affection ..." There was nothing about obeying. Years later Stephen said that they had secretly agreed that either one could end the marriage at any time.

Abby Kelley had found out the hard way how engrained was the prejudice against women. In 1840, already well-known on the Abolitionist lecture circuit, she was nominated to serve on the business committee of the American Anti-Slavery Society. The organization split down the middle because many red-hot Abolitionists were not ready to accord a woman the same rights they were demanding for male slaves. Some historians feel that the Abolition movement eventually worked against the women's rights movement, even though many reformers were active in both. The Abolition movement, which finally culminated in the Civil War, drained away most of the dedication and energy for other

52

causes. Not until the late 1860s did women's suffrage get put back on the front burner.

Another noted team in the struggle for Negro rights and women's rights was Lucy Stone of West Brookfield and her husband, Henry B. Blackwell. Theirs was another liberated marriage, even more so than that of the Fosters. Before the ceremony, which took place in West Brookfield in 1855, they issued a joint statement which said, in part: "we deem it a duty to declare that this implies no sanction of, nor promise of voluntary obedience to such of the present laws of marriage, as refuse to recognize the wife as an independent, rational being, while they confer upon the husband an injurious and unnatural superiority . . ."

Once married, Lucy Stone kept her maiden name and her own bank account, both radical innovations in the 1850s. One wonders what she would have thought had she lived to see the day when a woman would be named president of a Worcester bank. Ironically, when Massachusetts finally passed a law 30 years later allowing women to vote for school committee candidates, Lucy was refused a ballot because she would not register under her husband's name. Blessed with a remarkable voice and a powerful intellect, she was to be a major force in the women's liberation movement for almost 40 years. Susan B. Anthony said that she was converted to the women's rights movement only after she read the speech that Lucy Stone gave in Worcester.

What did the first Woman's Rights Convention accomplish? At the second Woman's Rights Convention, an even larger gathering held one year later at the auditorium in Worcester City Hall, President Paulina Davis noted that "Since the first Woman's Rights Convention was held, the doors of several Medical Colleges have opened with a welcome to the long-excluded sex; others have been established for women exclusively." Mrs. Davis also said that schools of design for women had opened in Boston and Philadelphia.

Ironically, that second convention saw Abby Kelley Foster move away from the mainstream of the women's movement. She angered the delegates by blaming women themselves in part for their plight:

"Let us, then, when we go home, go not to complain, but to work. Do not go home to complain of the men, but go and make greater exertions than ever to discharge your everyday duties.

"If women could be taught that the responsibilities devolved equally upon themselves and the other sex, they would seek out the means to fulfill those responsibilities. That is the duty we owe our daughters today; that is the duty each one owes to herself today, to see to it that we feel that we must enter into business, such as will bring in to the support of our families as much as the labor of our fathers, husbands, and brothers does. Woman's labor is as intrinsically

53

valuable as any other, and why is it not remunerated as well?"

That double message was not popular. Abby's was not a typical case. Her husband, Stephen, also a noted lecturer for Abolition and women's rights, believed so strongly in sharing labor equally in the home that he was bringing up their daughter at their farm on Mower Street so that Abby could continue lecturing around the country.

What else did the conventions of 1850 and 1851 accomplish? They sparked an interest in women's rights that did not die. In 1869, Sarah H. Earle's sister-in-law, Ann B. Earle, ran for a seat on the Worcester School Committee even though she could not vote, and won. Was she the first female elected official in Massachusetts?

In that same year, 1869, a Woman's Suffrage Convention was held in Washburn Hall. Ann B. Earle was elected a vice president and her husband, Edward, was elected treasurer. (Two years later he was elected mayor of Worcester to fill out the term of James B. Blake, killed in an explosion at the gas works.)

The main speaker at the 1869 convention was Julia Ward Howe. "The intervention of women in politics," she said, "her introduction into active life, is a new religion to all of us who believe in it."

The suffragist movement slowly gathered strength. In 1890, the Worcester Woman's Club was founded to push for women's suffrage and other causes. It hired Josephine Wright Chapman, a Boston architect, to design its splendid new building on Salisbury Street. Slowly public opinion began to shift. Wyoming had granted women equal rights, including the vote, in 1869, the same year as the Worcester Suffrage Convention. Other states, mostly in the West, followed Wyoming's lead. Finally, after years of suffragist agitation and demonstrations, on Aug. 26, 1920, the 19th Amendment to the Constitution was ratified. Women had the vote.

That was the end of one era and the beginning of another. Since then, the women's liberation movement has waned and waxed. It continues to advance in our own times, as women demand fairer treatment in ever widening fields. Progress sometimes seems slow; it was more than a century after Ann B. Earle was elected to the Worcester School Committee that a woman, Sara Robertson, finally was elected mayor of Worcester.

None of this would have surprised Lucy Stone and Abby Kelley Foster and those other intrepid women who met in Worcester in 1850. They knew from experience how hard it is to change human customs. The feminist movement of today is a direct lineal descendant of the woman's rights movement of the 1850s that got its momentum in Worcester's old Brinley Hall.

54

Chapter 13

Holy Cross and Its Ordeal by Fire

JULY 14, 1852, was a hot muggy day on Mount St. James. In a third-floor classroom, a teacher began burning old examination papers in a hot iron stove. By nightfall, the College of the Holy Cross was a smoking ruin.

The large college building, four stories high and about 200 feet long, containing classrooms, dormitories, faculty living quarters and dining facilities, was a wreck. Books, personal belongings, and furnishings that had been hurled from the windows lay strewn about the blackened hulk. Worcester firefighters, pumping water from the Blackstone River almost a quarter-mile away, were able to save only one wing.

The damage was estimated at $50,000. Holy Cross had no insurance. It did have a $12,000 debt. Although most of the library books were saved, the college never faced a grimmer prospect. It did not graduate a single student for the next three years.

At that moment and for weeks to come, the fate of Holy Cross hung in the balance. It was saved not because of the Jesuit authorities, but despite them. Or at least, despite Rev. Joseph Aschwanden, acting head of the Maryland Province, which then had jurisdiction over Jesuit activities in New England. Rev. Aschwanden immediately let it be known that the Jesuits wanted no part of rebuilding the college.

Holy Cross and its devoted faculty had survived a number of ordeals since 1843, when Bishop Benedict Joseph Fenwick of Boston had taken the academy founded by Father James Fitton six years before and turned it into the first Roman Catholic college in New England. College officials had gone through the ordeal of applying to the Massachusetts Legislature for a state charter — and had been turned down. The reason: Holy Cross excluded all but Catholics from its student body. If it had welcomed others, it would have opened itself to the charge of proselytizing.

The college had also gone through the agonies of building facilities, and hiring

55

faculty, and attracting students, all on a shoestring. The Jesuits had felt both friendship and hostility in the community of Worcester where nativist bigotry was on the rise, as it was in the rest of Massachusetts. (In 1855, and again in 1857, Worcester would elect Know-Nothing George Richardson mayor.)

In the weeks and months that followed the fire, the community rallied around. William Richardson, who owned the Worcester House, offered 30 of his rooms to faculty and students for the night at no charge. Several citizens offered accommodations in their homes. Fund raising soon got under way. As far as Worcester was concerned, rebuilding the college was a foregone conclusion and only a matter of time. The only real roadblock to the college's survival was a Jesuit. Father Aschwanden seemed adamant.

In vain did the irrepressible Rev. Anthony F. Ciampi, S.J., the new college president, say that he found "more life in the ruins of Worcester than in the whole of Frederick (Md.)." That may not have been the most diplomatic thing to say, but Father Ciampi, a native of Rome, was not known for diplomacy. He once wrote about the majority of his student body in unflattering terms: "The Irish stock brings the rudest and roughest kinds of beings — It takes much to lop and engraft them — to fructify."

Father Augustine Kennedy, a member of the faculty, wrote to Father Aschwanden in glowing terms of the bright prospects for the college. The wing that had been saved was a dormitory with 70 beds. There were rooms in the basement that could be converted to classrooms. The walls of the upper dormitory were still

FATHER JAMES FITTON

56

standing and could be quickly made part of a new building. The College could be rebuilt for not more than $10,000.

Father Kennedy noted the considerable achievements of Holy Cross, even then. Twelve of its graduates had gone into the Jesuit order (compared to only three from Georgetown). Also, noted Father Kennedy pointedly, if the Jesuits pulled out at this hour of need, the Bishop of Boston might never again let them into his diocese. But Father Aschwanden was unmoved.

Without the unflinching support of Bishop John B. Fitzpatrick of Boston, Holy Cross might have gone under. He found Father Aschwanden a tough nut to crack. At a meeting between the two in August 1852, the Jesuit offered to transfer the college, including its $12,000 debt, to the bishop. Bishop Fitzpatrick vetoed the idea. It would be a breach of faith, he said. It would be a black mark on the memory of Bishop Fenwick, who had put all his savings into Holy Cross. The bishop insisted that the Society's original acceptance of Holy Cross carried "at least an implied promise — that the Diocese should forever enjoy the advantages that result from the existence of such an institution." At that time, Holy Cross was the only Catholic college in New England.

In the end, it was the Holy Cross community and the people of Worcester who saved the college. Ordinary working Catholics of Worcester, many poor as church mice, donated their 50-cents and dollars. The alumni showed loyal generosity. Patrick Healy, son of an Irish immigrant and a Georgia slave, and brother of Bishop James Healy, donated $2,300 at a critical moment.

And, most important, many Protestants rallied to the cause. Despite the Know-Nothing mayor, despite the occasional spasms of anti-Catholic feeling that rolled across the state, Holy Cross had become a source of pride to the community, Protestant as well as Catholic. (A few years later, Isaac Davis, Alexander Bullock and Elijah B. Stoddard saw to it that the second Holy Cross petition for state incorporation went through the Legislature without a hitch.)

Nonetheless, for all this impressive support, the decision to rebuild was not made until April 4, 1853, after the Rev. Charles A. Stonestreet had replaced the stubborn Father Aschwanden as Jesuit provincial. After an offer of financial help from Bishop Fitzpatrick, Father Stonestreet gave the go-ahead. His one stipulation was that President Ciampi have $4,000 in hand before construction began. The money was collected by July — in only 16 churches.

The college had one more mortification to endure. That was the visitation of the "Nunnery Committee" of the Massachusetts Legislature. In those feverish times of Know-Nothingism, some politicians argued that the state should make sure that nothing seditious or rebellious or unpatriotic was going on at the various Catholic institutions in the state. So out went the "Nunnery Committee," headed

57

by Rep. Joseph Hiss. Hiss and his investigators visited Holy Cross during the first week of March 1855. In the dry words of Walter J. Meagher, S.J., and William J. Grattan, authors of "The Spires of Fenwick," the investigators "found no signs of treason, proselytism or other suspicions. An intensive probing of classrooms, dormitories, and closets throughout the halls turned up nothing subversive."

The committee gave Holy Cross a favorable report, but its antics at Holy Cross and elsewhere helped close out an embarrassing episode in our state's history. A few weeks later a legislative inquiry uncovered various indiscretions of the Nunnery Committee, including padded travel vouchers. On May 10, 1855, Hiss was expelled from the Legislature as "unworthy longer to occupy a seat on the floor of this House."

And so the long travail of Holy Cross finally ended. The college had survived fire, bigotry and near impoverishment. It had continued to function even after the state turned down its first application for a charter. It had triumphed over the efforts of the Jesuit provincial to shut it down.

In 1862, the state of Massachusetts made a gesture of symbolic importance when Gov. John A. Andrew attended commencement and handed out degrees to the 10 graduates. He was the first of many governors to do so. In 1964, President Lyndon B. Johnson visited Holy Cross and was awarded an honorary degree. The spirit of Bishop Fenwick must have been proud.

View of Holy Cross, circa 1880. The original building, left, was mostly destroyed by fire in 1852, and then rebuilt. Fenwick Hall, right, was built after the Civil War and later expanded.

58

Chapter 14

William Jankins and the Slaver

ON OCT. 30, 1854, a group of black men broke into a prison cell at Worcester City Hall and tried to lynch a white man.

Although the authorities rescued the victim in time, a mob of whites at the scene cheered the blacks on. They probably would not have lifted a finger to save the life of the man who was being stoned, clubbed and beaten.

The history books call it the Butman Riot, after U.S. Marshal Asa Butman, who was in Worcester to enforce a federal law. The law was known as the Fugitive Slave Act. Butman may have been looking for William H. Jankins, a slave who had escaped from his Virginia master 12 years before and had lived in Worcester ever since. According to the Rev. Albert Tyler, who wrote an account of the episode for the Worcester Society of Antiquity a century ago, Jankins "by industry had become a well-to-do citizen in the way of his calling." Rev. Tyler does not say what the calling was.

The news that Butman had arrived was proclaimed by the Worcester Spy in large type:

LOOK OUT FOR KIDNAPPERS!

BUTMAN THE KIDNAPPER OF THOMAS SIMS

AND ANTHONY BURNS IS IN TOWN

ACCOMPANIED BY ANOTHER OFFICER!!

THEY ARE BOOKED

AT THE AMERICAN TEMPERANCE HOUSE!

LOOK OUT FOR THEM!

59

That was not Butman's first foray into the North. Earlier in the year he had captured Anthony Burns, another escaped slave, in Boston. After an avalanche of abolitionist protest and near rioting in the streets, the case was brought to trial. Two artillery companies of militia, a company of U.S. troops and a company of Marines were brought into Boston to keep the lid on. Thousands, including 800 men from Worcester, carrying a banner inscribed "Worcester Freedom Club," marched in front of the courthouse. When the judge, bowing to the plain words and intent of the law, said that Burns would have to be surrendered into slavery, an insurrection almost broke out. By some estimates, it cost $100,000 to return that one slave to bondage.

Worcester Telegram & Gazette

The old City Hall, where U.S. Marshall Asa Butman was held in protective custody and where he was almost lynched by angry blacks.

60

The Burns case and others like it around the country lighted the train of powder that was to lead in seven years to Fort Sumter and the Civil War. Worcester was an abolitionist flashpoint, headquarters of Eli Thayer's Emigrant Aid Society set up to send free settlers into Kansas to save it from slavery. It had an influential group of Quaker reformers, including John Milton Earle, editor of the Spy. Its clergy had a long tradition of activism. The Woman's Rights Conventions held in Worcester in 1850 and 1851 had mobilized and energized various reform movements. And Central Massachusetts was the stamping ground of a whole cluster of radicals, including Stephen Foster, Abby Kelley Foster, Samuel May, Lucy Stone, Thomas W. Higginson and Sarah Hussey Earle. In addition, Worcester had no large textile industry to bind its Whig merchants to the South, as was the case with Lawrence and Lowell.

Perhaps not realizing any of this, Asa Butman set out for Worcester at the end of October, intent on capturing runaway slaves and returning them to Virginia in chains. Large bounties were paid for such exploits. A good slave was a valuable piece of property.

Jankins had been targeted by slave catchers at least once before. Shortly after the Fugitive Slave Law was passed in 1850, a man named Seabury came snooping around Worcester. But Jankins, alerted to the threat, stayed in hiding. He had friends.

Butman put up at the Temperance House, just as the Spy reported. Immediately, a committee of vigilance was appointed to keep a 24-hour watch on the hotel. There was much milling around in the street. The city marshal and the sheriff sized up the situation but thought things were under control. The mayor showed up, admonished the crowd, and went on home.

But somehow a confrontation was staged and Butman, by then thoroughly frightened, drew a pistol. A warrant was immediately issued and Butman was arrested for carrying a dangerous weapon and ordered to appear in court the next day.

Early next morning the mob began to gather, many blacks included. According to Rev. Tyler's account, when Butman came out of the courtroom he was confronted with a "Niagara" of denunciation. The crowd's mood was ugly. As Butman looked at "the many dark faces that lowered upon him . . . his spirit quailed before the vision and he begged of the city officers help and protection."

Butman was brought to City Hall and put in a room while a prominent politician spoke to the crowd in front of the courthouse, urging calm. But there was no calm inside, where three black men broke into Butman's room and proceeded to beat him up. They were stopped just in time and escaped through a window. Somehow, they were never identified or caught.

61

By then, the authorities were concerned mainly with preventing a serious riot and getting Butman out of town. They announced that Butman had agreed never again to come to Worcester. Under police guard, Butman was marched through the angry mob to the railroad depot. The police presumably did their best, but Butman was cursed, struck, tripped and stoned on the way. "The colored men especially, were almost beside themselves," writes Rev. Tyler.

Once at the station, the officials were chagrined to learn that the next train was not due for several hours. That was much too long. Things were getting too dangerous. Finally a hack was called and, protected by Stephen Foster, Thomas Wentworth Higginson and other noted abolitionists, Butman made his ignoble exit from Worcester. That was the last time anyone tried to enforce the Fugitive Slave Law in Worcester.

And William Jankins? According to Rev. Tyler, writing in 1878, "he is still with us, steadily and industriously pursuing his calling, as he has been through the many years since the attempt to kidnap him and carry him back to slavery. He had too many interests here and too much at stake to feel safe, after this attempt, and so he arranged the matter with his old master, obtained his free papers by purchase, and they are recorded in the office of the Clerk of the Courts — the only free papers ever thus recorded on the books of this county! Since the war, he has visited his old master, and from his lips learned the true inwardness of this attempt upon his liberty."

It's too bad that Rev. Tyler did not give a few more details to go with that somewhat puzzling last comment. But at least we know that Asa Butman did not carry William Jankins off to slavery, and that Jankins apparently spent many happy and productive years in Worcester after that dramatic episode at City Hall when free blacks and a slave chaser came face to face.

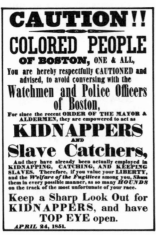

The Fugitive Slave Act set off a storm of protest throughout New England in the 1850s and helped push many people into the radical Abolition movement. Ralph Waldo Emerson and others vowed that they would not obey the law. The "Underground Railroad," which spirited slaves out of the South and into free Canada, was active in Worcester County.

62

Chapter 15

Mechanics Hall—
Almost a Fiasco

*I*T TOOK WORCESTER almost five years to build the Centrum.

It took Worcester 18 months to build Mechanics Hall, and that without a single power tool.

The difference was remarked upon more than once between 1977 and 1982, when everything that could go wrong was going wrong with the new civic center. By contrast, the golden years of 1855-57 looked like a piece of cake.

That would have astonished the men of the 19th century, for whom nothing went smoothly. Mechanics Hall had almost as many problems as the Centrum. It had construction problems. It started life as a financial fiasco.

In 1854, the Worcester County Mechanics Association, encouraged by Ichabod Washburn's offer of $10,000, finally got up its courage and voted to build a "Mechanics Hall." Ground was broken in July 1855 at a huge city celebration.

Those "mechanics" saw themselves as a new class who would use the tools of the industrial revolution to transform society. They were the builders, the toolmakers, the foundrymen, the blacksmiths, the carpenters, the stonemasons, the inventors, the wire makers and the machinists who were producing "from their workshops, more than six millions of dollars annually," according to an 1861 historical sketch of the association.

They had organized into an association in 1842, under bylaws written by Anthony Chase, county treasurer and a former shoemaker. Their first lecturer was Elihu Burritt, a blacksmith who had gained considerable fame by his mastery of literature, history, science and several foreign languages. In 1849, they held their first mechanics fair, a great success. But Worcester had no adequate hall. For several years, they talked about building one. Finally, in 1854, Ichabod Washburn's $10,000 moved them to a decision.

Things moved fast. A building committee was set up and Elbridge Boyden selected as architect. His fee was $600. Horatio Tower was master builder. The cost of a suitable building was estimated at $90,000, including land. Grand visions danced in people's heads.

63

Sidewalk superintendents were plentiful. So much so that Boyden complained to the building committee to get them off his back.

There were problems. After a heavy rain, a supporting foundation wall collapsed and had to be rebuilt. Despite all, the noble edifice slowly rose, exciting the community and inspiring news stories in the Boston newspapers.

In a way, Mechanics Hall was the Centrum of its day, but it won't do to stretch the analogy between the 1850s and the 1970s too far. The Centrum involved tax money, public credit and decisions by the city and state governments.

Mechanics Hall was a private venture by a state-chartered association. A tax exemption was the only claim it ever made on the public purse.

Yet there were interesting parallels. Mechanics Hall has been a public building from the start, open to practically everyone. For generations it was the intellectual and cultural center for most of Worcester County. Its pedimented cast-iron facade and cornice, soaring 86 feet above the sidewalk, dominated Main Street for generations. Its many activities attracted thousands of people and gave the central business district a shot in the arm, just as its builders said it would.

Mechanics Hall showed how courage and imagination, overriding doubts and fears, can stimulate a whole community to lofty achievements.

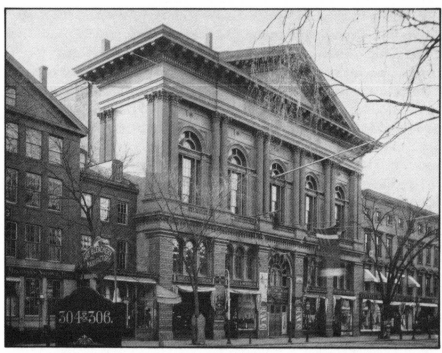

The Diadem of Worcester

64

But the big project had one disadvantage; it put the Worcester County Mechanics Association into bankruptcy.

The splendid new building was dedicated on March 19, 1857, amid pomp and circumstance that included the Boston Brass Band, the Worcester Light Infantry, two ex-governors of Massachusetts, dignitaries by the dozen, stirring speeches and excited throngs.

Oratory soared. A.H. Bullock said, "Let us dedicate this Hall in the broad and catholic spirit of modern art and culture. The mighty and beneficent enginery of the last 70 years is still in motion. The great historic procession has not passed by, but is ever on the grand march."

"We may well congratulate each other upon this achievement," said Henry S. Washburn. "Here it stands, and it speaks to you, today, in tones far more eloquent than I can command. Imposing and beautiful in its external elevation, the interior fills the beholder with admiration and delight."

Three months later, the holders of the third mortgage notes foreclosed when the association was unable to raise a few hundred dollars to satisfy some nervous creditors.

"The Association, once our city's pride," wrote one member, "by its begging has become an almost intolerable nuisance."

How did it happen? Were not the founding fathers of the Worcester County Mechanics Association practical men? How did they get themselves into such a bind?

They were practical men. Most of them had come up the hard way, from impoverished boyhoods.

But they also were visionaries. They wanted to change things. They wanted to improve the public school system so that the new generation would get off to a better start. They wanted to found a library, to hear lectures, to enjoy music, and experience the finer things of life.

Succeeding generations can be grateful that the association thought in expansive terms, but expansive meant expensive. By June 1857, the total cost was totted up at $162,000. Mechanics Hall, like the Centrum 125 years later, was almost 100 percent over budget.

That would have been a burden in the best of times, which 1857 was not. The city's businessmen, including many association members, were still trying to recover from the terrible fire of June 1854, which had almost wiped out the Union Street industrial shops owned and rented out to businesses by William Merrifield. The loss was estimated at $400,000. Then, in the summer of 1857, the country was hit by a financial panic brought on by speculation and overbuilding of railroads in the West. The stock market plunged. Bank credit and capital dried up. Although the 1857 Exhibition of Arts and Manufacturers, the first held in the new hall, was a great public relations success, there was not enough money in the till to pay for the medals.

At the peak of their success, the members of the Worcester County Mechanics Association had to suffer the indignity of seeing their splendid new hall taken over by foreclosure on the third mortgage.

It was a chastening experience. A committee was set up to find a solution. It discovered that the total debt owed — bonds, mortgages and notes — came to $104,000. There was general agreement that the building could not carry a debt of more than $50,000. Somehow, $54,000 of obligations had to be wiped out.

Into the breach stepped Stephen Salisbury. That was ironic, because Salisbury, landowner and real estate developer, was not eligible to join the Mechanics Association. (Neither was Levi Lincoln, lawyer and politician.) Salisbury offered to donate his $2,000 bond, plus $5,000 in cash if the total debt could be whittled down to $50,000.

Ichabod Washburn, the original benefactor of the project, agreed to assume $10,000 of the third mortgage, on the same terms. That gave the committee something to work on.

The compromise finally agreed to was for the bondholders to get 40 percent of par value for their bonds, and for the third mortgage holders to get $5,000 in cash for the $15,000 owed them. "After a persistent and strenuous effort, the compromise was effected on this basis," says the official account. One can well imagine. Nobody likes to take that kind of bath.

In the fall of 1859, the Worcester County Institution for Savings agreed to make a $50,000 loan to the association whenever all the other creditors gave up their claims in toto. On Dec. 10, 1860, the hall finally passed again into the hands of the Worcester County Mechanics Association, where it has remained ever since.

The hall has remained a community enterprise. That was proved in the 1970s when more than $5 million was raised to renovate it in spectacular fashion. At its 125th anniversary celebration in 1982, the old hall looked better than ever and ready for the next century.

There is a curious footnote to the Mechanics Hall story. In 1897, the association considered a six-story addition on Waldo Street to enlarge the capacities of the building. But then the venerable Elbridge Boyden took the floor to warn the association about the risks of going into debt. His eloquence carried the day and the idea was scrapped. Another 80 years would pass before the association finally voted for an addition on the Waldo Street end.

Chapter 16

The Great June Tornado – 1871

THE WORCESTER TORNADO OF JUNE 9, 1953, remains vivid in many minds. Tens of thousands of people still remember the terrible events of that eerie day.

A few people recall the Fitchburg tornado of July 17, 1924, which killed two people and wrecked whole sections of Fitchburg and Lunenburg.

But the tornado that struck Worcester County on June 11, 1871, has long been forgotten. Only a few faded newspaper clippings bear witness to its ferocity.

Like the 1953 twister, the 1871 storm traveled from west to east across Central Worcester County. The Aegis and Gazette, a weekly published by The Evening Gazette, gave a detailed account in its issue for Saturday, June 17, 1871. It said that the tornado the previous Sunday was first reported in North Spencer, although "it is probable that it passed over the north part of Ware, the south part of Hardwick and through Oakham before striking there." From North Spencer, the twister churned through Paxton, Holden, West Boylston, Boylston, Berlin and Clinton, where it apparently lost its lethal power.

The 1953 tornado originated in Petersham, tore through Barre, hopped 10 miles or so and came down in Rutland. It then ripped through Holden, North Worcester, Shrewsbury, Westboro and Southboro.

Powerful as it was, the 1871 twister was not a killer. The Aegis and Gazette did not report a single fatality. But it packed the same kind of punch as the howler that tore through Great Brook Valley 82 years later. Some of the accounts from 1871 read much like those from 1953.

Thus, in Paxton, it struck the barn of Nathaniel L. Parkhurst, "tearing it to splinters and partly unroofing his house. The barn of D.L. Ware, in the same vicinity, was also demolished. The house and farm buildings of John Warren, near Mrs. Ware's, had a wonderful escape. Nearly every tree on his premises, some of them within two feet of his barn, were uprooted and thrown a considerable distance, and although the trees were on all sides, the buildings were entirely unharmed."

67

In Holden, the windstorm struck the farm of Lewis Martin. "His house and barn are a complete wreck, nearly every joint in the frames being broken, so that nothing is left but a scattered mass of broken lumber. Mr. Martin and five children were in the house, and after the gale passed found themselves in the cellar considerably bruised, but not seriously injured."

The tornado then "crossed another valley, in which there was a pond, the water of which was whirled in the air and thrown forward for some distance in the path

Worcester Telegram & Gazette

The paths of two tornadoes. The Holden tornado of 1871 began in North Spencer and moved in an east-northeast direction to Bolton. The Worcester tornado of 1953 began in Petersham, curved down through Barre, Rutland and Holden through Worcester and then easterly to Framingham. The picture shows what it did in the vicinity of Burncoat Street.

68

of the gale. Next came a hill, just west of Holden center, surmounted by a heavy growth of pines. Through these the tornado swept, mowing them down like grass before a scythe, and leaving a track as clearly defined as if the work had been done by rule and line."

In the "village" of Holden, the storm created "indescribable havoc." Houses, barns and sheds were demolished or twisted on their foundations. The shop of H.D. Hubbard was "completely wrecked, hardly enough left for a bonfire." Three horses in an adjoining barn escaped with only slight bruises.

Then, "Crossing the county road to Worcester at this point, just south of the new cemetery, the gale struck the house of Ebenezer Parker, lifting it from its foundation, carrying it about its width and dashing it upon the ground with such force as to separate nearly every piece of lumber in it from its fellow. Mr. Parker and his wife were in the house, but escaped wonderfully, he having only an arm dislocated and she being somewhat bruised. The barn of John Burns was likewise demolished, but three of his children who were in it at the time, escaped uninjured."

The twister then crossed West Boylston near Malden Street but did less damage than in Holden. In Boylston it plowed up the ground "as if some mighty torrent had washed over it." But the main force seemed to be spent.

The wake of the storm displayed scenes of chaos like those so well remembered from 1953. "Near the barns destroyed the ground was strewn with fragments of carts, wagons, farming tools and the like, while near the dwellings furniture, bedclothing, curtains and clothing are twisted among the branches of the prostrate trees or scattered in broken and torn fragments for a long distance. In several places heavy timber fell across the highways and uprooted trees and broken fences are strewed in every direction."

The reporter noted something interesting: "Aside from the havoc in the path of the tornado, which was about ten rods in width, there seems to have been a force operating from each side, so that while the trees and other articles in its direct path are blown due east, many trees fell at the right and left at right angles with the main path, probably the result of the rush of air drawn in at the base, as that in the direct path was whirled upward, creating a vacuum."

The 1871 tornado was remarkable, first, for the amount of physical damage it wrought, and, second, for the lack of a death toll. The news accounts chronicle one miraculous escape after another. Even considering that Holden and the other towns were mostly empty fields and scattered farms, it is astonishing that not even one person was killed or badly injured.

Worcester County was lucky in 1871. Unfortunately, that luck didn't hold 53 years and 82 years later.

69

Two views of the aftermath of the great Lynde Brook flood in Cherry Valley.

70

Chapter 17

When Lynde Brook Ripped Cherry Valley

IN 1876, LYNDE BROOK RESERVOIR was the pride of the Worcester Water Department. It was built in 1863 and expanded in 1872, when the dam was raised 12 feet. When filled, it contained more than 700 million gallons of water.

It was filled to the brim in March 1876 after days of heavy rain. When anxious Water Department crews reported a leak, the engineers went up to the dam to look. Muddy water was gushing up through the floor of the lower gatehouse with such force that the gates could not be opened to relieve the pressure.

For almost a week, crews worked desperately to stanch the flow. Rocks, logs, gravel and bales of hay were dumped into the reservoir, but to no avail. Mayor Clark Jillson and his department heads visited the dam and argued about what to do. Some urged that a cut be made in the retaining dam on the east side of the reservoir. But Phinehas Ball, former mayor and the engineer who designed the dam, said that would lead to an uncontrollable torrent raging down Parson's Brook and into "New Worcester" (Webster Square). Hydrants were turned on in the city to relieve the pressure, but to little avail.

The surface of Lynde Brook Reservoir is 824 feet above sea level, about 120 vertical feet above Main Street, Cherry Valley. Fortunately, the people had several days to pack their belongings and move out of their threatened houses and mills. As the word of impending doom spread, the roads became thronged with sightseers who presented all sorts of problems. They swarmed over the dam and the side of the reservoir, they gave unsolicited advice and were a general nuisance for the harried officials, police and workers trying to save the dam.

At about 5 p.m. on April 1, water began oozing out of the bottom of the dam near the gatehouse. Faster and faster flowed the muddy stream while workers, city officials and rubberneckers scrambled to higher ground. In minutes, the stream became a torrent and then an angry geyser boiling out of the ground, cutting the gravel and earth like a knife. Quickly the hole widened, as huge chunks of dirt and rocks fell into the widening cavern. The lower gatehouse

71

collapsed into the swirling torrent. As the breach in the dam widened by the second, the upper gatehouse tumbled majestically into the flood. Three million tons of water went thundering down the steep gorge into Cherry Valley.

The people on the banks could hear a frightening rumble and roar as the surging water tumbled huge boulders down the declivity like bowling balls. Great pines and oaks were uprooted in seconds and carried downstream.

The torrent spread out when it hit the meadow at the bottom of the slope (Where Cherry Valley Lumber now is located) but slowed down hardly at all. Main Street, Cherry Valley, was turned into a river 400 yards wide. The flood carried away George Olney's barn and other buildings. It poured down into Smith's Pond, collapsing the 200-foot dam like "a barrier of bulrushes," according to the account in The Evening Gazette. The Smith textile mill was next. As the Gazette put it: "An L of the building melted into the yeasty waves like a house of cards, and all the smaller buildings extending out toward the stream followed down the stream." One wall remained standing. Except for the office safe, which miraculously stayed put, the mills were wrecked. Damage was estimated at $75,000 to $100,000.

Just below the Smith mill were two tenement houses. They were torn off their foundations and carried along on the angry waters like misshapen ships. Next was Wright Bottomley's satinet mill. In two minutes, not a trace remained. Below lay the mills of Ashworth & Jones, four stories of brick, "one of the finest in Cherry Valley." Two dams and several buildings were demolished. "Not a vestige of the boiler room is left," reported the Gazette. "The boiler itself was swept away and lies embedded in the channel half a mile below."

On plunged the wall of water, savaging the dams and mills of Hunt and Darling. The flood surged into Jamesville Pond, sweeping away 500 feet of Boston & Albany Railroad track.

At about 7 p.m., about two hours after the Lynde Brook Dam let go, the water began to rise in Curtis Pond. By 8 p.m., it was rising an inch every three minutes, and boards and debris began pouring over the spillway. Panic spread in the Webster Square area and many people set out for higher ground. By 8:25 it had overflowed the junction of Curtis and Leicester (now Main) streets and had reached the level of the bridge on Webster Street. Shortly after that, the bridge floated away and lodged against the side of the embankment.

Half an hour later, the Curtis pond dam gave away, releasing a flood that demolished part of the Curtis and Marble mill. A wooden section of the mill floated downstream and took away the Boston & Albany Railroad bridge. A tenement house owned by Curtis was moved out about 10 feet into the street. Further downstream, the Norwich & Worcester Railroad bridge was badly und-

72

ermined. Bridges on Southbridge Street were washed away. Parts of Millbury Street and Cambridge Street were under several feet of water, and many residents of Quinsigamond Village left their homes and spent the night outdoors on higher ground with bonfires to keep them warm.

The scene on the morning after was devastation. Cherry Valley was a no-man's land, strewn with huge boulders and rubble. Main Street was almost impassable. Smashed buildings, gaping cellar holes and tottering factories were strewn about with massive amounts of rubbish and litter.

Then came the sightseers. The Gazette estimated that 40,000 people showed up the next day to gawk. A special train of 10 cars was run from Fitchburg, and another from the Nashua and Lowell railroad, all crammed with passengers. "All available stage coaches, buggies and hacks were making frequent and productive trips from the center of the city to New Worcester, or as far up the valley as the Union House, and no job or lumber wagon was so clumsy that it could not be made of lucrative use by its owner," reported the Gazette. "The streetcars ran with doubled teams and their crowded loads amounted to fully 6,000 persons."

At one point in the day, 1,100 teams were counted passing a given point in South Worcester in one hour.

"Although there was some drunkenness in the crowd, and considerable rowdyism . . . the visitors were generally more orderly than might have perhaps been expected, and the officers had less trouble than they had apprehended," said the Gazette. The only serious accident occurred when a horse bolted, throwing Sgt. Francis Plunkett and his little boy to the ground. Plunkett was the armless Civil War hero of West Boylston whose portrait hangs in Mechanics Hall.

For all the damage, the human toll was light Either one or two persons disappeared during the flood and were believed drowned. The Gazette estimated the damage at $1 million. It would be at least $50 million today.

The city fathers, after talking with the indignant selectmen of Leicester, immediately made plans to rebuild the dam. The reservoir was the city's main source of water. The new dam was finished before the end of 1877, at a cost of about $230,000. Slowly the valley rebuilt. Today, standing in the lumberyard in Cherry Valley, one can hardly imagine that the tiny stream alongside once was a raging monster that did such devastation.

73

Baseball in some form had long been popular in America. In the 1880s, it became a craze. Professional teams popped up like mushrooms. Franchises were bought, sold and appropriated. The field above was at the Lakeview Oval on Coburn Ave. The Oval was opened by Horace Bigelow in 1891 as the headquarters of the Worcester Athletic Club, and was the center of the Worcester sports scene for many years.

74

Chapter 18

Sam Winslow vs. Mighty Casey

*W*HEN YOU THINK OF COMMUNITIES that have done the most for baseball, how high do you rate Worcester?

If you don't, you should. Worcester is no mean city when it comes to baseball history. It has a couple of credits that other places can only envy.

Forget about that triumph of public relations, Cooperstown, N.Y. Forget about the Abner Doubleday myth. Concentrate on important things, such as:

Where was the first perfect game pitched?

What pitcher struck out mighty Casey?

Those are the questions worth asking about.

Worcester, you should know, once fielded a team in the National League. During the 1880, 1881 and 1882 seasons, the "Worcesters" played their home games at a field off Highland Street, probably partly on land where the Worcester Tennis Club is located now.

It was there, on June 12, 1880, that Worcester pitcher J. Lee Richmond faced the Cleveland team and pitched the first perfect game that professional baseball had ever seen.

Although he struck out only five batters, not a single Cleveland batter made it to first base. Richmond always called it the first "no-man-reach-first-base" game. It was over in one hour and 26 minutes, and that included a rain delay of seven minutes. The score was 1-0. The Worcesters managed only three hits, one by Richmond, against the Cleveland pitcher.

The Evening Gazette was ecstatic about "Worcester's wonderful shut out of Cleveland." It was, wrote the sports reporter, "the best game on record. Their rivals did not secure a run, did not make a base hit, did not score a base run. In each of the nine innings the Cleveland batsmen were retired in one-two-three order, not a runner ever reaching first base. Games without base hits have been played, but a game without a base run is unprecedented."

Richmond, a senior at Brown University, was the regular pitcher for the Worcesters that season. The Worcesters played a season of 83 games, and Richmond

75

started in 66 of them. He finished the season with 32 wins, 32 losses and 57 complete games. After the Worcester team folded, he played for a couple of years with Providence and Cincinnati. His lifetime record was 75-100.

Some explanations are in order. In those days, the distance from the mound to home plate was 45 feet, not 60. The pitcher had to pitch underhand. What's more, the batter could specify whether he wanted a pitch in the high or the low zone, and the pitcher had to comply. A pitch outside the designated zone was called a ball. Eight balls was a walk.

Worcester Historical Museum

SAMUEL WINSLOW

Library of Congress

DEWOLF HOPPER

Worcester Telegram & Gazette

ERNEST THAYER

76

There was something else about Richmond. He said afterward that "my jump ball and my half stride ball were working splendidly that afternoon."

"Jump ball" is a phrase that catches the attention. Was Richmond the first pitcher to throw a curve?

Despite what you may have read elsewhere, he may have been. According to an article in the Brown Alumni Monthly years ago, Richmond once demonstrated his curve ball to a skeptical Brown physics professor who claimed that the alleged curve was an optical illusion. According to the story, all who watched were convinced that the ball curved.

So there you are: The first perfect baseball game in history. It happened right in Worcester. Somebody should put up a plaque.

Worcester has another claim to fame in baseball annals. It revolves around the famed epic doggerel, "Casey at the Bat," written by a Worcester man, Ernest L Thayer. De Wolf Hopper was the man who made it famous by reciting it thousands of times, but Thayer wrote it.

And who inspired him to write it? Why, Sam Winslow, that's who. Forget other versions you may have read about this bit of baseball history.

The story came out in 1894, when Hopper was appearing at the Worcester Theater in a play. As always, as an encore to whatever part he was playing, he was asked to recite "Casey." Sitting in the audience were Harry Worcester Smith and William Scofield, two Worcester men of note. They went backstage and asked Hopper to come over to the Worcester Club to meet Thayer, author of the poem. Apparently Hopper had never met Thayer and he readily agreed.

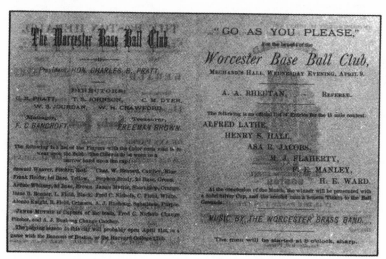

Worcester Historical Museum

The Worcester baseball team was recognized as a worthy cause a century ago.

77

The two got on famously. In a notable switch, Thayer recited the poem while Hopper listened. Hopper probably acted politely, but he later said it was the worst rendition of the poem he ever heard. Then Hopper asked Thayer a question that had been on his mind: What if anything had inspired the poem?

Thayer chuckled. "Sam Winslow," he said. He and Winslow, classmates who graduated from Harvard in 1885, had both been on the Lampoon. Winslow also was the ace pitcher for the Harvard baseball team, undefeated in the 1885 season. But during that season, Winslow had some scary moments. In three different games, he filled the bases in the ninth before he finally got the side out. The image of Winslow snatching victory from defeat at the last minute stayed with Thayer. The poem was published in the San Francisco Examiner on June 3, 1888. Shortly after, someone brought it to Hopper's attention, more or less as a joke. He claimed that, over the next 40 years, he recited it 10,000 times. It remains one of the most familiar verses in American history.

To be fair, there are other versions of the Casey myth. Daniel Henry Casey, who played for the Philadelphia Nationals way back when, always insisted he was the model. As the last man up in a crucial game, he whiffed, so he said. And there was another Casey — Daniel Henry — who was Thayer's classmate at Classical High. Late in life, Thayer wrote a letter suggesting that perhaps that Casey was the subliminal inspiration, even though he didn't play ball. Either way, the noted verse is rooted in an experience connected with Worcester.

So there you have it — the first perfect game in baseball history and the most famous poem ever written for any sport. Maybe the first curve ball ever seen in professional baseball.

Richmond, Winslow and Thayer. Why aren't they in the Hall of Fame? Why isn't Worcester noted in baseball circles? Is there no justice?

Chapter 19

Operator, Get Me Worcester

ON JULY 7, 1877, the Wellington Coal Co. installed Worcester's first telephone line between its Pearl Street office and Southbridge Street yard.

That was about one year and four months after Alexander Graham Bell, in his Boston workshop, spoke the first words ever transmitted by wire: "Mr. Watson, come here: I want you."

On Feb. 28, 1878, the Worcester Fire Department began installing telephone lines to its stations.

In December 1878, L.J. Knowles & Bro. of Worcester built a telephone line from its office to its factory in Warren, 20 miles away.

And on May 1, 1879, the Bell Telephone Co. rented an office in the Harrington Block and opened Worcester's first public telephone exchange, with 75 subscribers. Bell's great rival, Western Union Telegraph Co., opened its own telephone exchange in Worcester some weeks later.

The spread of the telephone after Bell's historic call was phenomenal. By June 1878, there were more than 10,000 Bell telephones in service. After it won a titanic patent fight with Western Union, the Bell Co. for more than 100 years held a virtual monopoly on one of the most universally needed devices of all time. By November 1879, there were 56,000 telephones in service, including 150 to 200 in Worcester. The first telephone operator, Emma M. Nutt, was hired by New England Bell Co. in Boston in September 1878. The first Worcester operator was Kittie Leland, hired a year later.

Bell, a quirky individual, wanted the standard telephone response to be "Hoy! Hoy! Hoy!" but that was not to be. Common sense prevailed. We can assume that Miss Nutt and Miss Leland answered with "Hello" whenever a customer buzzed the line.

Like all operators of that era, Miss Nutt and Miss Leland used footpower to ring up stations. A paper given by Frederick E. Waring to the Worcester Historical Society in 1910 notes: "In operating the first board, it was necessary for the

79

operator to tread her feet, as in running a sewing machine, to generate the ringing current used in calling a subscriber's station."

Telephoning on those early devices took patience. The same unit served as transmitter and receiver. According to one early bit of advice, "After speaking, transfer the telephone from the mouth to the ear very promptly. When replying to communication from another, do not speak too promptly . . . much trouble is caused from both parties speaking at the same time. When you are not speaking, you should be listening."

Not everybody was keen on the new idea. In Chicopee, a petition was presented to the selectmen to have the new telephone wires taken down. One commentator called the telephone a "scientific toy" of no practical importance.

But the telephone spread like sunlight over the land. By 1881, when American Bell Telephone issued its first annual report, there were more than 132,000 phones in use.

Worcester experienced the same frantic proliferation of phones that the rest of the country did. Within a year, there were four exchanges on the top floor of the Harrington Block, where Miss Leland was joined by three other operators. New England Telephone and Telegraph Co. was incorporated in 1883, absorbing 109 exchanges and 16,533 subscribers in Maine, Vermont, New Hampshire and Massachusetts, including 784 in Worcester.

Until 1891, telephone wires ran mostly over the tops of buildings, with the ground line being connected to Worcester water pipes. That system was doomed when the electric trolley cars began using the rails as a ground, making the telephone lines too noisy to use.

The first wire connection between Worcester and Boston was completed in 1880 but could be used only on Sundays. On other days, there was too much crackling interference.

The Worcester telephone system grew steadily. By 1893 it had 1,174 subscribers. In 1896 the company built a smart new headquarters on Norwich Street, and within 10 years it had more than 9,000 subscribers.

Along with the electric light company, the telephone company strung its wires ceaselessly, until downtown Worcester was draped in a maze of wires and cables.

By 1898, according to F.P. Rice's history of the city, "an automatic signal multiple switchboard" had been set up at the Norwich Street exchange.

"This switchboard system, which enables the subscriber to call the office by simply removing the telephone receiver from its hook, and which automatically signals the office when the communication is finished, is considered the ideal telephone system and is being introduced in other large cities of the United States."

Before that, according to Waring's paper, "on the first switchboard the operator had to walk the entire length of the board in order to complete a call for the subscriber whose line was the last one on the switchboard. On the present board, an operator can call any subscriber without leaving her chair."

The Worcester telephone system and New England Telephone Co. went on to ever-greater things. In 1930, the company moved its headquarters from Norwich Street to a brand new building on Elm Street. The surrealistic long lines center on Main Street was built in 1974. Always there were more new customers to service and more new services to offer. American Telephone & Telegraph Co. became the most gigantic corporation in the world.

On Jan. 1, 1984, one chapter of the amazing saga was closed. After long court hearings on monopoly charges, AT&T was broken up into various subsidiaries. Worcester residents were enfolded into something called "NYNEX," a holding company operating telephone services in New England and New York.

NYNEX, itself an $18 billion corporation with almost 100,000 employees and 10 million customers, is only one part of the huge system that grew from Alexander Graham Bell's inventive genius.

As Bell himself might say, were he here to see it: "Hoy! Hoy! Hoy!"

Worcester Telegram & Gazette

The Worcester telephone switchboard office, circa 1896. The cubicle in the corner, partly obscured by a post, is a pay station booth.

81

All eyes were on the clock of the Old South Church, then located on the Common, when Worcester went on U.S. Standard Time. In the rear is the newly-constructed Chase Building complete with tower. The tower was later removed

82

Chapter 20

When Time Moved Backward

O N NOV. 17, 1883, sharp-eyed readers of The Worcester Evening Gazette noted an unusual item:

"The regulator in Mr. A.F. Burbank's jewelry store at No. 241 Main Street, from which Mr. George W. Harlow strikes the 12:15 stroke on the fire alarm bells, was set back 15 minutes 44 seconds at noon today; and the stroke at 12:15 tomorrow will be struck by the regulator. When this stroke is struck, clocks that have not been touched will point to 12:30 o'clock or a little later."

Worcester, along with the rest of the United States, was about to go on U.S. Standard Time.

The next day, Sunday, Nov. 18, 1883, tens of thousands of eyes all over the country were fixed on the clocks on city halls, churches, banks, etc. In hundreds of communities, as the public clock minute hands were shifted forward or backward, people changed their clocks and watches accordingly. In Boston, the clocks were put back 16 minutes; in Washington, D.C., ahead by eight minutes.

On Monday, for the first time in history, church bells and factory whistles from Maine to the Carolinas (except for a few temporary holdouts) announced the arrival of noon at about the same moment.

Standard Time, with regular time zones across the country, had been a dream of the railroads since at least 1852, when The American Railroad Journal published an editorial endorsing the idea. Railroad timetables were becoming a nightmare as they tried to accommodate the many varieties of local time.

For centuries, people had set time by the sun. Noon was supposed to be when the sun was directly overhead. As a result, train travelers journeying from Boston to St. Louis were constantly resetting their watches. The time in Cincinnati might be 20 minutes different from the time in Chicago, and both different from the time standard of that particular railroad. By 1880 there were more than 50 different railroad times.

The idea of regular time zones across the United States and Canada, varying from each by exactly one hour, was developed largely by Charles F. Dowd,

83

principal of Temple Grove Ladies Seminary in Saratoga Springs, N.Y., and Sandford Fleming, a Canadian. William F. Allen, secretary of the General Railway Guide, kept hammering away at the idea with railroad executives, who finally agreed to go along.

Convincing local and federal officials was another matter. The mayor of Bangor vetoed a City Council ordinance endorsing standard time. In Washington, when the secretary of the Navy ordered all government clocks shifted to Standard Time, the attorney general overruled him on the ground that changing time was a prerogative of Congress.

In Worcester, the mayor and City Council studiously avoided endorsing the new-fangled idea, despite the pleas of Gazette editor Charles Doe, a strong proponent of Standard Time. "The sun itself is a very a poor time-keeper," said one Gazette editorial in explaining the vagaries of the earth's eccentric orbit.

As the momentous day approached, Doe ran a string of editorials and articles explaining the change and what it would mean. "The idea of such a radical change is somewhat disturbing to conservative minds," he wrote, "but practically, we fancy the subject will be forgotten in a week."

On Saturday, Nov. 17, on the eve of the event, the Gazette did its best to prepare the masses. The trains, it said, would all be on Standard Time tomorrow at noon.

Starting Monday, said the Gazette, the schools would be on Standard Time and all the school clocks would be reset "in conformity with the dial on Old South Church." It noted that the Old South and First Unitarian Church clocks would be reset to Standard Time "at noon, Sunday."

Also, "Mr. O. Blake & Son have prepared a circular explaining the new time arrangements, which they are distributing among the public schools."

As Doe predicted, the day came and went smoothly. On Monday, the Gazette reported that "At the Union Station, the event was one of much importance for railroad employees, and almost 100 of them assembled to witness the introduction of the changes and set their watches when the signal came from Boston. There was considerable excitement and interest manifested, and there was no hitch in the arrangements. Jewelers who have been busy for a fortnight past answering questions from the serious, were on hand at their stores yesterday and were beleaguered with questions. Many people who had not stopped their watches previously were puzzled about the propriety of setting the hands back, and delayed making the change. Watchmakers say there is no harm in setting the hands back, if the watch is in good order."

The only dubious note was sounded by a man who said that the first day of Standard Time seemed longer than usual.

And so the new era came to Worcester, the United States and Canada. Within a few weeks or months, the last holdouts, including Bangor, had adopted the new system. Time continued to march on, but in more regular ranks and files than hitherto.

Worcester Telegram & Gazette

The clock of the First Unitarian Church on Court Hill also was set to the new standard time on Nov. 18, 1883.

E.B. Luce

BIGELOW'S GARDEN

Bigelow's Garden, including the Rink, had its heyday in the 1870s and 1880s, when the roller skating craze swept the country. For 20 years, it was the most popular spot in Worcester. It was torn down around the turn of the century to make way for the Telephone Co. building and other commercial structures.

Worcester Telegram & Gazette

HORACE BIGELOW

86

Chapter 21

Worcester at the Rink

IN THE 1980s, everybody knows that the big action in Worcester is at the Centrum.

In the 1880s, everybody knew that the big action in Worcester was at the Rink. It was the Centrum of that era, and then some.

The Rink, or Bigelow's Garden, as it was sometimes called after Horace H. Bigelow acquired it and expanded it, is long gone. But in its heyday, from 1878 into the 1890s, the huge wooden structure was jumping two or three times a week. Whatever was available in the line of popular entertainment was featured at the Rink — band concerts, plays, operas, marching bands, pageants, expositions and roller skating.

Especially roller skating.

The Rink stood between Foster and Mechanic streets, a stone's throw from where the Centrum stands now. Alfred, Eugene and Charles Lalime, skating promoters from Canada, built it. It measured 225 feet by 100 feet outside. Inside it featured a rink 70 feet by 175 feet, big enough to accommodate 500 or more skaters. Around the rink was a promenade 15 feet wide. Leading into the main arena was a large entry room with restrooms, a ticket office, a skate room and a vestibule. This was a big time operation. Worcester was about to succumb to the roller skating madness that was sweeping the country from coast to coast.

James Plympton of New York was the man who first put America on wheels. After he invented the modern roller skate in 1863, he and the country went on a spectacular roll. Plympton's skate clamped onto regular shoes, much like the old-fashioned ice skate. It was ideal for the Yuppies of the Gilded Age. Roller skating did not depend on ice, it could be enjoyed by women as well as men, it provided thrills and spills and it was satisfyingly exhibitionist.

Plympton, who began his career abroad, patented his roller skate in Europe and the United States, and then sold franchises for skating rinks in France, Australia and the Dutch East Indies before he returned to the United States in 1876. His Brooklyn skate factory turned out 2,000 pairs of skates a week, but couldn't keep up with the demand. In 1876, he began to farm out skate orders to manufacturers, particularly the Winslow Skate Company of Worcester. Samuel Winslow had made thousands of pairs of ice skates, and had no trouble switching to roller skates. In the next few years, he made more than 20,000 pairs of roller skates for Plympton.

Through his patented monopoly on roller skates, Plympton gained a monopoly on skating arenas as well. Those promoters who wanted to use his skates had to buy franchises. The skates were leased from him and a percentage of the rentals turned over to him. The Lalime brothers had to negotiate a deal with Plympton before they could open the Rink for business.

It opened on Dec. 20, 1878, in a dazzling dedication. Mayor Charles B. Pratt and the full Board of Aldermen and the Common Council were there. Everybody who was anybody was there. The Gazette reported that the hall was lighted by "kerosene and gasoline, three chandeliers hanging from the center of the rink. The building is partly heated by four stoves, two placed at each side."

"Professor" Peter Kynock, a professional skater, was on hand to help timid females and clumsy males get their skate legs. William Field of Boston was in charge of the skate room. He fitted eager customers with rental skates and kept the skates in repair.

The hall was spectacularly decorated with flags and bunting, red, white and blue. The mayor made a speech. Then out came the trained skaters, led by Kynock. And then the ordinary people rolled onto the floor. The Gazette reported that more than 200 were wheeling around the arena at a time, with relatively few mishaps.

Two hundred was one of the smaller numbers recorded. In the days and weeks ahead, as the skating frenzy spread, crowds or 400 and 500 were reported. The Lalimes went from triumph to triumph. On Jan 29, 1879, the Rink hosted Continental Night, an occasion of no mean proportions. The Lalimes, eager to build a rink in Fitchburg, had invited the whole Fitchburg city government as guests. The whole Fitchburg city government came, too. There were more speeches and another skating exhibition by Kynock.

In the weeks that followed, the Gazette had two and three stories a week about goings-on at the Rink. The Centrum, in all its glory, never intoxicated the community quite the way the Rink did in those first years of the skating frenzy.

There was one jarring note that the Gazette reported. Two men, John Potter and John Kennard, said that they had bought tickets to the Rink and had been refused skates.

They were black.

They brought suit against the Lalimes. The case was heard by a Judge William-

88

son. A.G. Lalime was vague on why the men had been refused skates when there still was plenty of room in the arena. He said he couldn't recall anything said about color of skin. After hearing the testimony and pondering it for a couple of weeks, Williamson ruled that the defendants owed each of the plaintiffs $1 and court costs for breaking a contract. However, he added that no civil damages could be awarded for "mental suffering."

The case was one of the first in Worcester courts that referred specifically to "civil rights."

Encouraged by the success of the Rink, the Lalimes expanded to other cities, including Springfield. But they overextended themselves to the point where they needed a cash infusion. Enter Horace Bigelow, one of the great entrepreneurs of Worcester history. Bigelow had made a lot of money during the Civil War manufacturing shoes for the Army on an assembly line basis, sometimes using prison labor. He invented shoe machinery that was exhibited at the Vienna Exposition in 1873, where it astonished the Emperor Franz Joseph with its speed.

Back in Worcester and out of the shoe business, Bigelow began to buy up land around Lake Quinsigamond and develop it for summer recreation. He bought the "dummy" railroad that ran from Washington Square to Lake Quinsigamond and used it to run excursion tours between downtown Worcester and the lake, thus giving the masses easy access to that great recreational resource. Bigelow, a wealthy entrepreneur, was something of a populist plutocrat. Most of his ventures were aimed at improving the lives of ordinary men and women. Eventually, he gave the city most of what is now Lake Park.

Early in the 1880s, Bigelow bought four failing Massachusetts skating rinks, including the Worcester Rink. A.G. Lalime stayed on as manager. Bigelow was a born promoter and he brought in a dazzling array of entertainment — operas, plays, symphonies, bands, indoor polo, sports events, religious rallies, political conventions, six-day bicycle races and exhibitions. He put in a public swimming pool, a carousel and other attractions and named the complex "Bigelow's Garden." It fronted on Norwich Street and encompassed the whole block between Foster and Mechanic streets.

Roller skating remained popular for several years, but Bigelow chafed under the franchise system that Plympton had set up. He thought it ran counter to the goal of providing "wholesome entertainment for the hard-working people at prices within their reach." He and Sam Winslow decided to break the Plympton roller skate monopoly. On Jan. 6, 1880, the day Plympton's patent expired, Winslow began manufacturing roller skates of his own design. At about the same time, Bigelow stopped paying franchise fees to Plympton and lowered admission prices at his rinks, including the one in Worcester. He even allowed customers to use their own skates for a small fee.

Bigelow went all-out on the promotion. He organized skating competitions with prizes of up to $150. He put on all manner of extravaganzas, theatrical productions, political conventions, fairs, exhibitions, athletic contests and whatnot. The Rink was a livelier place than ever.

Plympton could do little about the Rink, but he sued Winslow on the grounds that an 1866 patent for improvements to his roller skate was still valid. But Winslow's lawyers produced evidence that a skate much like the 1866 model had been in existence before 1863, the date of the original patent. Judge John Lowell of the U.S. Circuit Court in Boston ruled in favor of Winslow.

Plympton did not give up. Armed with new data, he appealed to the U.S. Supreme Court. Before the case came to trial in 1887, Winslow agreed to pay Plympton the nominal sum of $500 for his rights as the "original and only inventor" of the roller skate. But by then it was all academic, because the 1866 patent had run out, too.

Thus did two Worcester men break the great roller skating monopoly, an event widely hailed as a victory for democracy and the common man.

Like many another fad, the roller skating craze peaked and then declined. Bigelow found a new enthusiasm — electricity. In 1887 he staged the first electrical exhibition in Worcester, complete with the first electric trolley car. He built the first electric power station in the city, and later sold it to the Worcester Electric Light Company. He became convinced of electricity's therapeutic powers. At a demonstration at the Rink, customers suffering from arthritis and rheumatism were invited to sit in a special electric car, where the electricity current was supposed to ease their pain. Some reported feeling better, some said they felt no different.

After 1890, the Rink's popularity waned. A "Dictionary of Worcester" published in 1892, called the Rink "a place of popular amusement much frequented during the past few years, but whose glory has now departed." In 1897, it was divided and rented out. The A.S. Lowell Co. ran a millinery shop in part of it. Eventually it was torn down to make way for the new telephone company building and other structures on Norwich and Foster streets.

But in its prime, the Rink — part of Bigelow's Garden in its later years — was the place that everybody was talking about and going to. It was almost a century before the people of Worcester got that excited about any other building.

Chapter 22

The Telegram vs. Grover Cleveland

PRESIDENTIAL ELECTION campaigns don't have to be boring, notwithstanding the dreary affair of 1984.

Take the campaign of 1888, when a Worcester minister called President Grover Cleveland a rogue and a wife beater, causing a national ruckus and inspiring an indignant letter of rebuttal from Mrs. Cleveland.

The Worcester minister was the Rev. C.H. Pendleton, pastor of First Baptist Church, then located on Main Street near Ionic Avenue. He had returned from a visit to Washington, where he had heard the gossip about the White House, including the sad situation of poor Mrs. Cleveland, whose mother reportedly had been packed off to Europe to get her out of the president's hair.

Cleveland, the first Democrat in the White House since the Civil War, was intensely hated by Republicans. The Telegram was one of the rock-ribbed, 200-proof Republican newspapers that seldom missed a chance to attack him and ridicule him.

In his first presidential campaign in 1884, political enemies revealed that Cleveland was the father of an illegitimate child. The Republican campaign slogan, chanted up and down the country, went as follows:

Ma, Ma, where's my Pa?

After the election, the Democrats countered with:

Gone to the White House, ha, ha, ha.

Cleveland's GOP rival in that campaign was James G. Blaine, who also inspired a ditty by the Democrats:

Blaine, Blaine, James G. Blaine,

Continental liar from the state of Maine.

The campaign was dirty and hard-fought. It may have been decided by four words that have gone down in American political lore. One of Blaine's supporters, a New York minister, gave a speech in which he called the Democrats the party of "Rum, Romanism and rebellion." Blaine lost New York by a hair, and Cleveland went to the White House.

91

GROVER CLEVELAND

FRANCES CLEVELAND

REV. C.H. PENDLETON

AUSTIN P. CRISTY

Presidential campaigns of the last century were extraordinarily vicious. Candidates were often accused directly or by innuendo of thievery, stupidity, indecency and immorality. This particular episode in the 1888 campaign was not out of the ordinary.

92

Once in the White House, Cleveland married a woman almost 30 years younger than he was. By all impartial accounts, it was a good marriage. Cleveland was a devoted husband and father. But the yellow Republican press, including the Telegram, would have none of that. Austin P. Cristy, publisher of the Telegram, ran Rev. Pendleton's revelations in a story headed:

OUR NATIONAL WIFE BEATER

The Telegram quoted Rev. Pendleton at length. Cleveland was "the very incarnation of a barroom politician." He was "an individual of the grossest propensities and of mediocre ability intellectually." His "riotous conduct does not stop at the bare relation of a drunken frolic, but goes further and tells of his abusive and insulting conduct to Mrs. Cleveland; such abuses and such insults as are not confined to mere talk but are expressed by blows."

These reports came from "high authority," according to the Telegram's story, and "are far from idle rumors; and the only reason they have not been sent broadcast over the country before is the extreme delicacy which the merest allusion to them in the newspapers involves."

Extreme delicacy was not a strong point of the Telegram under Cristy, a foe of all Democrats, especially low-tariff ones.

Summing up, the Rev. Pendleton was quoted as saying: "Can such a man be fit for the high office of president of the United States? I am sure that Grover Cleveland is the very last man I would vote for."

The story was picked up by the wire services and published across the land. The Democrats and the Democratic newspapers were furious. The Boston Globe, Democratic to the core, sent a reporter to Worcester to interview Rev. Pendleton. He apparently denied most of what the Telegram had printed, including all the liveliest parts.

"I made no such statement," Rev. Pendleton told the Globe reporter about the wife-beating allegation. "Nor did I ever hear that such was the case. The reporter of the Telegram, William Walsh, wrote up the conversation I had with him from memory, and made me responsible for statements that I not only utterly despise, but am profoundly sorry for, humiliated and ashamed of.

"Mind you, I well knew of the reputation of the Telegram as an unscrupulous sheet, and had taken pains to remind him several times — that what I was saying was not for the public, and he expressed his assent."

Was Rev. Pendleton shocked when he read the account in the Telegram? inquired the solicitous Globe reporter.

It "made me so sick," replied Rev. Pendleton, "that I could not eat any breakfast."

The Globe did not stop there. Somehow it got hold of a letter written by Mrs. Cleveland to a Mrs. Marguerite Nicodemus, who worked in a valentine shop on Front Street. Mrs. Nicodemus had written Mrs. Cleveland for her comments on the Telegram story. The Globe published both letters a few days later. Mrs. Cleveland's comments were indignant:

> *I can only say that every statement by Rev. C.H. Pendleton in the interview which was read me is basely false, and I pity a man of his calling who has been made the tool to give circulation to such wicked and heartless lies. I can wish the women of our country no greater blessing that that their homes and lives may be as happy, and that their husbands may be as kind, tender, considerate and affectionate as mine.*
>
> *Frances Cleveland*
> *Executive Mansion*

Cristy was livid. He launched into a volcanic attack on the Globe, a newspaper he had no use for, anyway.

"The Boston Globe — is, and for years has been, a disgrace to journalism," he wrote in a lead editorial. "It is the organ of Boston's hoodlums, the champion of rum sellers and of rum shops. It is the defender of municipal thieves. It is a perverter of local and general news, and has cultivated the art of lying about events and men to a perfection that is notorious among newspapermen from Boston to Texas."

After a long chronicle of the Globe's transgressions, Cristy zeroed in on the Pendleton affair:

"The sublimest fake of all was yesterday located in Worcester. It is in the shape of an interview with Mr. Pendleton. Mr. Pendleton knew he was being interviewed by a faker and preserved a discreet silence. From the few words which he dropped, the young man went home and in the garret of the building, which the Globe does not own, where its editors write up their telegraphic news from all over the world, he faked a lengthy story of what Rev. Mr. Pendleton said. The striking feature was in what Mr. Pendleton did not say. He was grossly misrepresented in his statement by the Boston Globe, as every other honest man has been who has been interviewed by the Globe's representatives."

Cristy asserted that the Telegram's version of what Rev. Pendleton had said was true, and that the Globe version was a pack of lies. He also accused Rev. Pendleton of acting strangely and making "erratic statements." Cristy attributed this to Rev. Pendleton's being hounded by reporters from Democratic newspapers "whose only purpose is to misquote him."

94

Who was lying and who was telling the truth? More precisely, which version was closer to the facts of the matter? Did Rev. Pendleton indiscreetly tell the Telegram reporter more than he later admitted, perhaps in the belief that he was speaking off the record? Did the Telegram embellish and sensationalize the interview? No one will ever know for sure.

This may sound like a bit of insignificant froth on the great river of history. But consider this: Grover Cleveland lost the election of 1888, even though he actually got 100,000 more votes than Benjamin Harrison did. Despite that majority, Cleveland lost enough big states to come up short in the electoral college. (Four years later, in 1892, Cleveland ran for a third time and won, the only comeback president in U.S. history).

Can it be that the Rev. Pendleton's unguarded comments, republished across the land, swayed enough voters for Cleveland to lose the 1888 election? Was a Worcester Baptist minister responsible for giving the nation those four unforgettable years of Benjamin Harrison?

Alas, we will never know. What we do know is that presidential campaigns used to be a lot more free-swinging and entertaining than they are now.

Before the Wachusett Reservoir dam was built, the railroad ran on a trestle across the valley. Along with everything else, the railroad had to be relocated.

96

Chapter 23

West Boylston's 'Day of Doom'

IN FEBRUARY 1898, Augustus Harper of West Boylston dragged a dead horse to the "horse cemetery" on Thomas Harlow's land near the Nashua River and left the carcass on the ground until the spring thaw. Before long, an official of the Metropolitan Water Board was at Harper's door, demanding that the carcass be removed. Harper must have been amazed; people had always dumped their dead animals at Harlow's horse cemetery. No more, said the man from Boston; the water board owned the property and pollution of the river would no longer be allowed.

As the Worcester Telegram reported about that time, the townspeople of West Boylston were belatedly waking up to the fact that the "day of doom" was approaching. Things would never be the same.

The new era had begun in 1893, when the Legislature authorized the state Board of Health to find the best way to provide Boston with more water. When the engineers concluded that a great reservoir could be built by damming the south branch of the Nashua River at Clinton, West Boylston Center's fate was sealed. Within 15 years, 25 to 80 feet of water would cover the land on which sat the common, the town hall, the hotel, the stores, four schools, three churches, four factories, 157 homes and dozens of farms.

Many more homes eventually were taken to protect the watershed. The 486 dwellings on the West Boylston tax list in 1896 had shrunk to 250 by 1905.

West Boylston in 1894 had a total assessed valuation of $951,000. The property earmarked by the state for taking had an assessed valuation of $558,000 — almost 60 percent of the total.

Forty years later, thirsty Boston would undertake an even more spectacular project in the Pioneer Valley, where it wiped out four towns and built the Quabbin Reservoir. That huge undertaking has overshadowed the building of Wachusett Reservoir. But at the time, Wachusett was probably the biggest construction project ever attempted in Massachusetts. Its impact on West Boylston was immense and lasting. Had the reservoir not been built, the town probably

97

would be Worcester's largest neighbor, with perhaps 40,000 people.

It didn't happen all at once. The state came in, bargained with homeowners, and bought one house after another. In many cases, the people were allowed to live in their homes rent-free until the time of demolition. State surveyors continued doing their work and town residents were warned that certain time-honored practices no longer would be allowed. No more animals would be dumped in Harlow's horse cemetery. No more kitchen and bathroom effluent would be allowed to drain into the river. Youngsters would no longer swim in Oakdale Pond. The state wanted the Nashua River made pristine as soon as possible. Although the enormous dam and reservoir were still years in the future, work was going ahead on a huge nine-mile aqueduct from Clinton to Southboro.

On March 14, 1896, The Evening Gazette warned of some of the sociological implications. Worcester, it said, should get ready for the influx of the roustabouts who would be doing the heavy work on the job. For one thing, the city should follow the example of Clinton, which had decided to close down all its saloons for a year. Although "the better class of men" would be handling the horse teams, there would be others to do the heavy lifting, "and with the hangers-on, the riff-raff of society, a plentiful toughness will be present in the camps."

With the river diverted through an aqueduct to Southboro, the footings for the dam were laid. Construction took several years.

The Gazette said that "The common laborers receive $1.50 a day" or $9 a week. Of the nine dollars, "from $3.50 to $4.50 goes for board and a bunk in a shanty. A dollar a week is sufficient for clothing and tobacco. The remaining three or four dollars goes for whiskey, and generally very hard whiskey, of the kind that has concealed in its bottles impulses to fight or stab or shoot, according to the imbiber's nature, which generally means his nationality."

Work went ahead, presumably with some excitement at night. On March 9, 1898, the Telegram reported that the gates had been opened at Clinton shortly after 10 a.m. and that the water had arrived at the eastern end of the aqueduct three hours later, flowing pure and clear and headed for the new Sudbury Reservoir.

In those years, West Boylston center gradually disappeared. One by one, the busy mills closed and were demolished. St. Anthony's Catholic Church, the Congregational Church and the new Baptist Church all were sold. As a sentimental (or maybe political) concession, the state allowed the abandoned Baptist Church to remain standing next to the water's edge. It stands today, a sort of defiant gesture by a town submerged to Boston's thirst and greed.

The houses gradually emptied as their former owners found or built new homes. Some people moved their houses to new locations. The first to do so was William A. Burns, who jacked his house up, put it on huge sleds, and used 14 horses to drag it to its new location on Scarlett Street.

By Jan. 17, 1906, the 25 abandoned buildings remaining in the old town were sold at auction, bringing prices ranging from $26 to $102. The famed Beaman Oak, 20 feet around at the base, was felled and carted away to the sawmill. The wood was used to finish the ladies' parlor in the new Congregational Church. The Beaman Burying Ground was moved, with all its inhabitants, to a new location, an undertaking that required the signatures of all 117 extant Beamans.

Meanwhile, the Boylston Construction Co. was stripping the loam, brush and vegetation from thousands of acres of West Boylston's fields, woods and meadows. More than 230,000 cubic yards were gouged out, carried up to two miles by a small railroad and dumped into a fill 300 feet long and up to 70 feet high — the foundation of what is now Route 12 across the reservoir. The regular railroad that ran through the center of town was moved, tie by tie and rail by rail.

Much of the brawn for the construction was supplied by several hundred laborers recently imported from Italy. Although many of those workers' descendants are now among the town's leading families, there was culture shock in West Boylston 90 years ago. The town was made up mostly of Yankee Baptists and Congregationalists, with a sprinkling of Irish and French Canadians. Both West Boylston and Clinton were dry, a notion that the Italians found ridiculous. Not

99

only did the Italians drink, they also gambled. They lived jammed into the abandoned houses or in huts they built themselves.

According to West Boylston historian Helen Maxwell Hamilton: "In 1904, the Boylston Construction Company, which had the contract for stripping the basin, arranged, in an attempt to keep its Italian employees contented and satisfied, a huge celebration of the Feast of the Assumption. On Sunday afternoon, Aug. 14th, the Marine Band of Rodi, Italy, arrived at the railroad station and marched through the town to French Hill where a huge white tent containing an altar and a shrine to the Virgin Mary had been erected. There they gave a band concert which was followed in the evening by a religious service, fireworks, and dancing. On the following day there was a festival of sport. Many of the non-Italian residents were on hand to watch the greased pole contests and the chase of the greased pig. Nothing like this was ever seen, before or since, in West Boylston."

As construction proceeded, the town was plagued by drifters and tramps, just as The Evening Gazette had warned. Some of them came looking for work, others to cadge meals by one means or another. The town poor farm had to put up 10 to 15 tramps every night. In 1897, the state officials converted an abandoned business block into housing for transients. It accommodated as many as 300 tramps a month.

Gradually, the town center was moved up to high ground. Churches and town buildings were rebuilt around a new common, which actually once had been the original common. The drastic drop in taxable property and tax revenue was partly made up by the Metropolitan Water Board, which agreed to pay the town $12,000 a year in lieu of taxes forever. There were other financial agreements.

When the gates were finally closed at the new dam in Clinton, the enormous empty basin, stripped of all greenery, began to fill. For months the townspeople of West Boylston watched the water slowly rising, obliterating all the familiar landmarks, burying what had been the town center under 63 billion gallons of water, in some places more than 100 feet deep. When the great reservoir was at last filled in 1907, the heart of West Boylston had vanished forever. Gone were the busy mills, the farms, the shops, the hotels, the schools, the puffing trains, the horse-drawn wagons, the children playing in the fields, the people going to church services on Sunday mornings. Only the empty Baptist Church on the shore remained as a symbol of what once had been.

100

Chapter 24

When Worcester Was Almost Motown

MANY YEARS AGO, at the turn of the century, Worcester had a humming auto industry turning out engines on an assembly line basis.

One of Worcester's automotive pioneers was John C. Speirs, manufacturer of the Speirs and Lovell Diamond bicycles. Speirs was a gifted mechanic and inveterate tinkerer. In 1895, he and Charles Fletcher produced Worcester's first or second car — an electric runabout. According to an article in Worcester Magazine in 1908, "The propulsion was an electric motor, and power was generated by 40 special accumulator cells. the car was designed to carry two people; the wheels were equipped with 4-inch tires, and it . . . was run at a maximum speed of 20 miles an hour . . ."

The other candidate for Worcester's first motorist was Ralph L. Morgan, who reportedly was driving some sort of contraption around the city's bumpy streets possibly as early as 1894. Morgan's car was described as "a steam-driven vehicle, with a small gas-burning boiler under a seat which was fastened on a shaky body with 4 bicycle wheels. It had a tiller and crude steering apparatus, but he drove it successfully and the resulting reputation took him to Pope-Toledo as chief engineer."

Speirs stayed in Worcester and kept experimenting. Two or three years later he brought out a second automobile, this one a steamer. In March 1900, the Locomobile Company of America, headquartered in Orange, leased Speirs' old bicycle factory, hired him as superintendent, and tooled up to produce engines for its popular steam car, built on patent rights bought from the Stanley Brothers.

On March 25, 1900, the Worcester Telegram published an account of what was going on:

"Within two weeks the old Speirs bicycle factory, Nebraska Street, will be transformed into a gigantic engine factory capable of turning out daily 50 4 ½ horsepower steam engines for the Locomobile Co. of America . . . The business of the company has expanded. There are now 70 men in its employ in the Worcester factory. Within two weeks 150 more machinists and skilled mechanics will be setting up engines . . ."

101

The Telegram reported that Locomobile had also bought the Humber bicycle factory in Westboro to manufacture "running gear and all body parts and equipment." Worcester would build engines and water tanks. The car itself would be assembled in Bridgeport, where Locomobile had another plant.

The chassis, said the Telegram, was "the original Stanley carriage, which has been pronounced by experts about the perfection of development of steam driven carriages . . . When the water tank is filled for a run of 25 miles, it weighs 550 pounds."

In those days, steamers were as common as gasoline engine cars, and some engineers predicted that the future belonged to steam, not gasoline. Several Worcester men, including Ralph Morgan, Charles Crompton, Edward P. Sumner, Frank G. Dwight Jr., George Rockwood and Alonzo G. Davis were driving steamers or gasoline autos around Worcester before 1900. In 1900, 20 Worcester cars took part in the McKinley campaign parade down Main Street. When number plates began to be distributed in 1903, Davis got number 6, the lowest ever given to a resident of Worcester. He kept it until he died in 1950.

The Locomobile was powered by steam produced by a gasoline burner. It took only five minutes to get the pressure up to 150 pounds, at which point "all the automobilist has to do is to jump aboard and he is ready for a 25 or 30 miles without a stop . . . And it looks easy."

American Antiquarian Society

The Locomobile dealership moved from Pleasant Street to Main Street shortly after the turn of the century. The Locomobile, partly manufactured in Worcester for a few years, was popular in this area.

102

At the end of his interview, the intrepid Telegram reporter climbed into a Locomobile for what apparently was his first automobile ride "and with his fate and his story in the hands of Frank L. Dwight was whirled to Only square. Mr. Dwight appeared to pay less attention to his machine than the ordinary road driver would to manipulating a whip and handling the ribbons over a horse."

Locomobile built more than 3,000 engines in Worcester before it moved the operation to Bridgeport. The first automobile agency in Worcester was a Locomobile agency, located first at 87 Pleasant St., later at 671 Main St.

Although the company's stay here was brief, it may have had a lasting effect on industrial Worcester. Thanks to an order from Locomobile, Wyman-Gordon Co. forged its first auto crankshaft in 1902. And in 1905, the world's first machine for grinding crankshafts and camshafts was ordered by Locomobile from Norton Company. Those two orders may have given Wyman-Gordon and Norton a foothold in what was to become the most important industry in the United States.

Worcester had other connections with the budding auto industry. Winslow T. White, manufacturer of the White steamer, was a Worcester Polytechnic Institute graduate. So was Elwood Haynes, inventor of the Haynes automobile. The Stanley brothers of Stanley Steamer fame had business links with Locomobile for a time. After Locomobile moved to Bridgeport and switched from steam to gasoline engines, the Stanleys began to make their famous line of steamers.

The Worcester County Agency of the Locomobile Company of America, located at 87 Pleasant Street about 1900, was the first auto dealer in Worcester.

American Antiquarian Society

103

Ralph L. Morgan designed the engine that powered the Pope-Toledo car and also manufactured a heavy chain-drive truck about the time of World War I.

Worcester never became a Detroit or Flint, but it produced a number of gifted tinkerers and inventors. In addition to Speirs, Morgan, White and Haynes, there was Jerome Wheelock, designer and manufacturer of heavy steam engines. A Wheelock truck driven by compressed air was advertised in 1904, but little else is known about it.

The Worcester Automobile Club was founded on Feb. 16, 1901, following the McKinley parade. One of the moving spirits was W.J.H. Nourse, a Canadian who had served with "Chinese" Gordon in the Sudan. The club was incorporated in 1905, John P. Coghlin, president. By 1908, it had 500 members and elegant quarters on the 5th floor of the Chase Building on Front Street. The club still flourishes as the Bancroft Auto Club.

In those days, automobiles were started with hand cranks. George Jeppson was the first Worcester motorist to suffer a fractured arm caused by the crank kicking back. Percy Whittall was the second. The medical profession had a name for the ailment — Fracture of the Radial Styroid.

Cranks, arm fractures, the Locomobile and 2,200 other makes of cars have long since vanished. But the memory lingers on.

Chapter 25

The 'Yankees of The East'

ON JULY 14, 1901, the Rev. Albert W. Hitchcock spoke at the cornerstone-laying of a new church in Worcester.

"We look upon you," he said, "as a new Pilgrim bound to our shores to find religious freedom and liberty of conscience. We look upon you as a sort of dividend for what we have invested in foreign missions in Turkey . . . It is no small thing to have a colony of these 'Yankees of the East' in our city."

The church was the Armenian Church of the Martyrs on Pink (now Ormond) Street. It was the first Armenian Congregational Church and possibly the first Armenian Protestant Church in the United States. It was a way station on an extraordinary pilgrimage.

The Armenians were only one of the many ethnic and religious groups that came to Worcester in the last century, but their story is one of the most unusual. They came from remote Asia Minor. They seemed to have little in common with either the older settlers or the newer immigrants of Worcester. One might have expected them to join the teeming masses of immigrants in New York or Philadelphia or one of the other big coastal cities, but not a small inland community.

Why Worcester? Why did Armenian families living in places like Kharpert and Hussenig, 5,000 miles away, think first of Worcester when they made plans to emigrate? Why did an Armenian at Ellis Island at the turn of the century insist to an immigration official that he had not yet arrived in America because "Worcester is America?" Why did Worcester at that time have more Armenians than either New York or Boston? And why did Rev. Hitchcock liken them to Yankees?

According to Dr. H. Martin Deranian, historian of the Armenians in Worcester, there were various reasons. First, there were the missionaries. In the 1880s and 1890s, Worcester sent at least four missionaries to Turkish Armenia. Rev. Crosby H. Wheeler was the founder and first president of Euphrates College in Kharpert. His daughter, Emily, taught there. The Worcester missionaries became caught up in the drama and tragedy of the Armenians, Christians since earliest times. By the 1870s, they were struggling to maintain their faith and identity in

105

the face of increasingly savage persecutions by the Muslim Turks.

The second attraction was Worcester industry, then undergoing pell-mell growth. Philip Moen, president of Washburn and Moen Manufacturing Corp., which was to become the largest wire mill in the world, was a churchman interested in the Asia Minor missionaries. Judged by modern standards his wire mill

Worcester Telegram & Gazette

The Armenian Church of the Martyrs on Ormond Street may have been the first Armenian Protestant church in the United States.

106

was a grim sweatshop, but it provided the Armenians with a foothold in a strange and hostile land. By 1889, 265 Armenians were on the payroll, mainly as wire drawers. Worcester then had about 700 Armenians.

The first Armenian arrived in the 1860s, but did not stay. Like many others, he worked for a while in Worcester and then returned to his native land. The first one to settle permanently was Hovhannes Yazijian, also known as John Writer, who arrived in 1877. In 1882, he sent for his wife and children. In that year, the 18 Armenians in Worcester used to gather at the Yazijian home on Beacon Street for prayer meetings and religious services. As the colony grew, the services were moved to the Summer Street Protestant Chapel. For that one brief period, Apostolic and Protestant Armenians worshipped together, but the ecumenical spirit did not last long. By 1889, they had divided into three different religious societies, each with its own pastor. The first Armenian Apostolic service in America was celebrated at the Reform Club Hall on Main Street, Worcester, on July 28, 1889. The Church of Our Saviour on Laurel Street was consecrated on Jan. 8, 1891.

Life was hard in Worcester for the Armenians. The other immigrant groups harassed them and waylaid them. Foremen in the wire mill extorted money from them for the better jobs. Other ethnic groups considered them non-Christian or even "Turks," the most bitter insult. Since they were willing to work for practically nothing, they were considered scabs. They had nothing to do with unions or workmen's associations or any organization run by non-Armenians.

But all those difficulties they endured as sojourners in a strange place. Unfortunately, they were not united. They were bitterly divided by age-old political and religious schisms that they had brought from their native land.

On March 27, 1893, the Worcester Telegram ran a lurid, front-page story.

"BLOODY RIOT IN CHURCH OF OUR SAVIOUR ON LAUREL HILL" was the headline.

It described a wild free-for-all in which more than 100 Armenians, including the Rev. Hovsep V. Sarajian, pastor, smashed furniture, fought in the streets and committed general mayhem. A police wagon arrived but no arrests were made, even though several men had broken noses and blood running down their faces.

What was the cause of the brawl? The Telegram made it out to be a clash of personalities, but it was much more. It involved the accusation that Michael Topanelian had informed the Turkish ambassador to Washington that some Worcester Armenians took a "revolutionary attitude" toward the Turkish government.

That made Topanelian out to be a traitor, which was unlikely. More likely, the issue was a religious difference. Topanelian was a believer in the Apostolic Church of Armenia and he was disturbed by the trend toward Protestantism that

107

he saw among his people. Only a tiny minority of Armenians in Armenia were Protestant but, thanks to the missionaries, the percentage of Protestant Armenians in Worcester was far higher — perhaps 20 percent or more.

The fight on Laurel Street had many complex roots, but it clearly marked the splits that were developing in Worcester's Armenian community. Despite Topanelian and his best efforts, the Protestants continued to worship and recruit members.

During those years, some Armenians remained ambivalent about Worcester and America. A surprising number returned to the old country, despite the increasing Turkish repression. In 1895 came a terrible massacre, in which more than 100,000 Armenians are said to have perished. That helped convince many Armenians that their future lay here rather than back in Harpoot. Still, some returned, regardless. Most perished in the Armenian genocide of 1915, when, according to some observers, 1.5 million died at the hands of the Turks.

But for those who stayed, America at last began to fulfill its promise. Apostolic or Protestant, Armenians began to become Americans and share in American life. They became doctors, lawyers, businessmen, politicians, writers, movie producers, artists. They became the "Yankees of the East" even while they scattered over the United States, from coast to coast.

Wherever they may find themselves, the chances are good that Armenians in America still have an ancestral memory of Worcester, Mass. For many of their ancestors and relatives, Worcester was the original golden door.

Chapter 26

Elbridge Boyden's Last Hurrah

ELBRIDGE BOYDEN WAS WORKING LONG HOURS during the winter of 1897-1898. Along with his son, Mason, he was designing a new front and a major addition to the old courthouse on Court Hill.

A few months previously, Boyden had lost out in the bidding to design the new Worcester City Hall. Undeterred, he plunged into the competition for the new courthouse job. He also was making plans to bid on the design of a new bridge across Lake Quinsigamond.

Boyden, almost 88 years old, was still ambitious, energetic and full of plans and ideas.

Born in Somerset, Vt., in 1810, Boyden had been apprenticed to a carpenter. At night, after work, he taught himself the principles of architecture. He had established a construction business in Athol before he came to Worcester in 1844 to work on an addition to the "Insane Asylum" on Summer Street. In 1847 he went into partnership with Phinehas Ball, later mayor of Worcester. Over the next 50 years, Boyden developed a reputation as the dean of Worcester County's architects, designer of more buildings than even Stephen C. Earle, his friend and younger contemporary.

Boyden is best known for his masterwork — Mechanics Hall, a building of such extraordinary elegance and acoustics that it became something of a national landmark even before the Civil War and remained one 125 years later. He also designed St. Paul's Cathedral, the Spencer Congregational Church and an extraordinary number of buildings throughout New England and beyond.

He designed churches in Athol, Wilbraham, Ware, Oxford, West Brookfield, Gilbertville, Northfield, Rutland, Leicester, Dudley, Winchendon, Ashburnham, Brattleboro, Vt., Saratoga, N.Y., Keene, N.H., Rutland, Vt., Newport, R.I., West Randolph, Vt., Littleton, N.H., and Williamsville, Conn.

He designed at least eight Worcester schoolhouses and schools in Fitchburg, Gardner, Athol and Brookfield. He did buildings for Nichols School in Dudley, Worcester Polytechnic Institute, Worcester Academy and Cushing Academy. He

109

did town halls for Sutton, Gardner, Orange, Southboro, and Upton.

He designed a courthouse for Fitchburg and one for Warren County, N.Y. He did major design work on jails and houses of correction in Fitchburg, Greenfield, Worcester and New London, Conn. He designed the state "Lunatic Asylums" at Taunton and Tewksbury. When the Providence & Worcester Railroad was built, he designed all the depots from Uxbridge to Worcester. He designed hotels, he designed houses. Elbridge Boyden had left his mark on Worcester County and places far beyond.

Now, in the evening of his life, Boyden wanted to achieve one last big success, and the new Worcester County Courthouse seemed like the right place at the right time. Most of the leading architectural firms — Earle and Fisher, L.W. Briggs, Fuller, Delano and Frost — were competing for the prized plum. As Boyden and many others understood it, the goal was to preserve the old courthouse, including the classic front portico.

He proceeded accordingly, designing two wings to complement the existing facade in a harmonious whole.

But in January 1898, the county commissioners awarded the contract to another architectural firm, Andrews, Jacques & Rantoul of Boston. The firm's plan was for a brand new courthouse which meant the demolition of the old one, including the facade.

Worcester Telegram & Gazette

The Worcester County Courthouse as it looked in 1898, before it was partly incorporated into the current Courthouse. The 1876 addition by Stephen C. Earle, at left, still stands as part of the Courthouse.

110

The community — or at least an influential segment of it — was outraged. On Jan. 27, 1898, the county commissioners held a public hearing to hear a debate on the proposed design. Stephen Salisbury was there. So was Stephen C. Earle, who had designed the south addition (still intact) to the courthouse in 1878. They were joined by a cluster of prominent citizens who presented a petition urging the county commissioners to reject the Andrews, Jacques & Rantoul plan in favor of Boyden's.

John R. Thayer said that the new design should be dropped because it would result in an unsatisfactory structure. Col. W.A. Gile gave his opinion that the old courtroom was the best in the commonwealth and should be preserved intact. Speaker after speaker poured scorn on the plans and urged they be dropped in favor of Boyden's.

Then it was Boyden's turn. According to the Evening Gazette, he "spoke at some length." Among other things, he said it was a shame that the commissioners had chosen the "poorest of all the plans submitted." He said it would be a mistake to eliminate the classic front of the old courthouse.

But the commissioners were in a bind. They already had signed the contract and were bound to pay Andrews, Jacques & Rantoul $15,000 in architectural fees and supervision costs. District Attorney Herbert Parker said that it was a serious business to break a contract.

Worcester Telegram & Gazette

The Courthouse as it looked when first completed. The old American Antiquarian Society building stands at the right.

111

In the end, the county commissioners decided to go ahead with their plans. But the old courthouse was spared, at least in part. According to John Herron, local architect, the lovely facade was taken down and the front moved back. But the columns were saved and incorporated into the new courthouse front. The south wall of the courthouse was preserved, along with the 1878 addition designed by Earle. The courtroom inside is much the same as it was when built in the 1850s.

The current courthouse has become so familiar that Worcester County residents now hardly give it a thought. But at the time, some felt that its flat, squat appearance seemed uninspired compared to the older building.

Boyden quickly turned to a new challenge — the proposed new bridge to replace the unsightly causeway across Lake Quinsigamond. He remained as busy as ever. On Friday, March 17, he attended a reunion of the Worcester County Mechanics Association and was his usual lively self. The next day, while at a meeting of the Worcester County Society of Architects, he became ill and was taken to his home on Harvard Street. He died there on March 25, 1898. His last words were, "That will make a fine bridge."

Chapter 27

Worcester's First Catholic Mayor

WORCESTER HAS HELD some election cliffhangers since it got its charter in 1848, but none to surpass the first one of the 20th century.

The campaign for mayor in December 1900, was the only one in history to end in a tie — 8,061 votes for Democrat Philip J. O'Connell, 8,061 votes for Republican William A. Lytle.

The special election the following February was won by O'Connell, the first Irish Catholic to become mayor of Worcester. His victory was the kind of breakthrough on a local level that the nation experienced 60 years later when John F. Kennedy was elected president of the United States. Politics in Worcester would never be the same. But then, the city already had changed more in the previous 15 years than some thought possible.

Worcester had come roaring into the 20th century at full throttle.

The 1900 Census showed that the city topped 100,000 population for the first time.

Worcester had a brand new City Hall that had cost $650,000, complete with furnishings. It was the pride of the community.

The last of the horsecars had been put out to pasture and replaced by the new electric trolleys.

The gaslights and kerosene lamps were giving away to electric lights.

Worcester was fast becoming one of the industrial powerhouses of New England. It had an integrated steel industry complete from blast furnace ingots to piano wire. Its hundreds of factories turned out an awesome array of products, from grinding wheels to looms.

Its endless demand for labor attracted people from far and wide. Irish, French-Canadians, Swedes, Italians, Poles, Lithuanians, Greeks, Armenians, Jews, Assyrians, blacks, English and others were drawn to Worcester as if by a great magnet.

Row on row of new three-deckers climbed the hills and provided homes for workers. Between 1848 and 1900, the city population soared from about 15,000 to more than 100,000.

113

Despite these considerable changes, things stayed pretty much the same at City Hall. For all those 52 years, Worcester had been run by the established business and industrial interests. From Levi Lincoln in 1848 to Rufus B. Dodge in 1900, all the mayors were Protestant. Since the Civil War, most had been Republican.

The 20th century meant change. It was only a matter of time before someone would be able to forge a coalition to challenge the Yankee dominance. Given the numbers, the Irish most likely would lead the revolt.

PHILIP J. O'CONNELL

WILLIAM A. LYTLE

CHARLES NUTT

The city election of 1900 was a turning point in Worcester history. City politics would never be the same.

114

Philip J. O'Connell was not the first Catholic to run for mayor. That distinction probably belongs to Andrew Athy, who challenged Samuel Winslow a dozen years before. When Athy threw his hat into the ring, he was working at the Winslow Skate Company. He was promptly fired and went into the funeral business. Although Athy was to have a long career in politics — he is said to have won more than 30 elections for city council, board of aldermen, state legislature and other posts — he never made it as mayor.

Some people doubted that 1900 was a good year for any Democrat to run for mayor of Worcester — let alone an Irish Catholic Democrat. The country was in a Republican tide. William McKinley had just been swept into the White House. Worcester had been strongly GOP for years.

Yet, in the national election, the Democrats had held onto their Worcester district congressional seat when John M. Thayer defeated Charles G. Washburn. The Republicans were split over that, and recriminations were in the air. The city GOP, led by Aldus Higgins, was unable to repair the breach in time.

On Nov. 26, the GOP caucus nominated William A. Lytle, a clothing store owner, for mayor. It was a mistake. Although Lytle had been active in Republican politics for years, he was disliked by many in his own party.

Still, few observers gave O'Connell any shot at winning. Not only was he Catholic, he was only 30. The Worcester Evening Post, traditionally Democratic, dismissed him as an ambitious lightweight with no chance of winning. "It is only a question of Lytle's majority," the Post sniffed editorially.

The Telegram, ferociously Republican, dismissed O'Connell as "a smiling blank."

The Gazette was kinder. It commended O'Connell's "keen wit and quick tongue" as well as his "sound judgment and common sense." But it concluded that "Mr. O'Connell cannot be elected to the office of mayor."

Not for the last time, the newspapers were wrong. They all underestimated their man.

O'Connell was young, but he was no lightweight. He was a rising young lawyer who had gone through Boston University Law School in three years, graduating magna cum laude. He was a skilled debater and an experienced politician for all his youth.

He set about organizing his campaign, appealing to as wide a variety of voters as possible. He appointed a committee of 25 to help get out the vote. His organization proved effective beyond most expectations.

O'Connell may have been helped by another factor — the liquor issue. The periodic question of licensing the liquor dealers was on the ballot, and the dries, including a number of Protestant clergymen and the Worcester Telegram, were

115

demanding an end to the "rum houses." The liquor interests, plus thousands of ordinary folk, rallied to the principle of freedom for drinkers.

A large vote was guaranteed. On election day, more people voted on the liquor question than voted for mayor.

Election morning dawned to the tune of confident predictions from the GOP camp, despite worries about possible defections. When the ballots were counted that night, Lytle was declared the winner by 41 votes. The Republicans went to bed astonished that they had done so poorly but relieved that O'Connell had been defeated.

The following morning, City Clerk E. H. Towne, tabulating the official count, discovered an error in Ward 5, Precinct 1. Lytle's vote there had been counted as 268 but was only 208. There followed days of recounts, growing tension and excitement in the newspapers. Finally, on Dec. 18, came the announcement:

Lytle, 8,061.

O'Connell, 8,061.

O'Connell decided to challenge three ballots disqualified by the registrars. But on Jan 7, 1901, the Massachusetts Supreme Judicial Court, Chief Justice Oliver Wendell Holmes presiding, ruled for the registrars and against O'Connell. The tie vote stood.

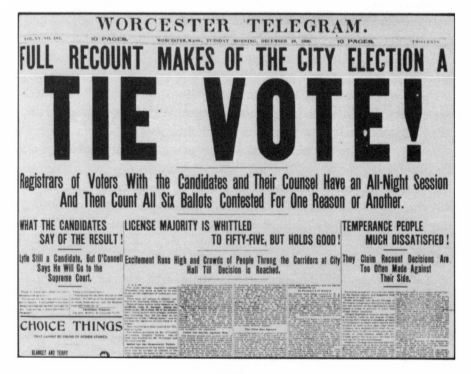

116

That meant new party caucuses, new nominations and a new election. The Democrats rallied unanimously behind O'Connell again, but the Republicans gave Lytle the nod only reluctantly. The split in the party was widening.

A hot campaign followed. The Democrats, realizing they had a chance to win at last, set out with a vengeance to enroll new voters and rally the faithful. The Republicans, aghast at the prospect of losing control of City Hall, did the same. More than 1,000 new voters were registered in the space of two weeks.

The newspapers, reasonably fair during the first campaign, showed more partisanship the second time. The Telegram was particularly one-sided. O'Connell was repeatedly linked with the "rum-sellers," and the Democratic campaign tactics were reviled.

"DOUBLE CONCAVE-CONVEX FALSEHOODS TO FIT ALL OCCASIONS" read a Telegram headline a week before election. The story made some extraordinary charges against O'Connell and the Democrats. O'Connell headquarters, said the Telegram, had spread the lies that Lytle had stolen $3,000 from the Masons, had kept dogs and cocks for fighting, had repeatedly failed in business, was anti-Semitic, was Jewish and was an inveterate gambler at the Commonwealth Club.

There is little reason to believe that the O'Connell people ever made such charges. Austin P. Cristy, the irascible Republican publisher of the Telegram, was not noted for restraint. His campaign against O'Connell was vituperative. He was venomous against Republicans said to be abandoning Lytle and going over to the enemy camp. Cristy was not above manufacturing issues for political purposes.

The front pages of the Telegram and the Worcester Spy, another Republican paper, showed crass favoritism:

"IF EVERY REPUBLICAN IN WORCESTER VOTES THE O'CONNELL MEN WILL BE OUT OF SIGHT TONIGHT" blared the Telegram.

"EXPERIENCE AND PROVEN ABILITY IN PRIVATE BUSINESS AND CITY AFFAIRS MAKE W.A. LYTLE, REPUBLICAN CANDIDATE, THE BEST EQUIPPED CANDIDATE FOR MAYOR" proclaimed the Spy.

With headlines like that, who needed editorials?

Alas for the GOP. O'Connell carried the city 9,559 to 9,048 for Lytle. It was the largest vote ever cast for mayor. It was, of course, an all-male vote. Women would not vote for mayor for another 18 years.

O'Connell had won a sensational victory but his time in power was brief. Hardly a day after his election he was confronted with demands from the Democratic City Committee to make certain appointments to the License Board. He resisted. The party split. Nine months later, O'Connell was soundly defeated for re-election by Edward F. Fletcher. He never ran for public office again. In 1915, he was

117

appointed a judge of the Superior Court, a position he held until his death in 1931.

Nevertheless, O'Connell's tenure as mayor was a landmark. The Spy graciously said it marked "the end of political bigotry" in Worcester, which was an overstatement but revealing.

Many years later, O'Connell's son, Attorney Laurence O'Connell, spoke at the unveiling of his father's portrait at the Worcester County Courthouse. He told how Philip O'Connell's parents, "two immigrants from Ireland," saw their son inaugurated as mayor of the city. "This election must have seemed in its place and time . . . something like the election of John F. Kennedy 60 years later," he said.

O'Connell's victory set off recriminations among Republicans. The Spy and the Telegram, each blaming the other for the GOP loss, went after each other hammer and tongs. Charles Nutt, who later wrote a history of Worcester, was editor of the Spy. One of his editorials provoked a typical response from Cristy:

"CRAZY CHARLIE NUTT IN HIS PENDULUM ACT" was the Telegram headline. The news story went on to say that "Charlie Nutt seems to have entirely lost his head. It never was a star head but now it's a goner." The story went downhill from there.

A few days later Nutt struck back. In large type and on the front page of the Spy he printed an anonymous letter charging that Cristy was secretary "of the first and most violent A.P.A. organization in Worcester."

The American Protective Association was a notorious nativist and anti-Catholic organization that flowered around the turn of the century. The charge of anti-Catholicism and A.P.A. membership dogged Cristy for years.

True or false? Who knows at this late date? Judging from some of the stories Cristy printed during his 35 years as owner and publisher of the Telegram, the charge is believable.

Considering everything — the blatant appeals to ethnic votes, the rumors, the misrepresentations, the prejudice — Worcester came through its new test reasonably well. Things certainly were no worse than they were in some parts of the country in 1928, when Al Smith ran for president.

Professor Vincent Powers, a student of Worcester's political history, once said that O'Connell's election was a definite breakthrough. "It was a landmark," he said. "A kind of invisible barrier came down."

It was a chapter in the never-ending process of what used to be called "Americanization."

118

Chapter 28

Emma Goldman vs. Police Chief Matthews

THE WEEK OF SEPT. 5, 1909, was one hot news week in Worcester. The city editor of the Worcester Telegram must have scribbled furiously in his assignment book.

Just two days previously, the wire had brought the breathtaking news that Dr. Frederick Cook had reached the North Pole.

Two days later, the wire brought the equally breathtaking news that Robert Peary had reached the North Pole — and had found no trace of Cook's alleged visit. The North Pole controversy would be erupting in the headlines for years.

Then there was that big conference of brains up at Clark University, where President G. Stanley Hall had assembled savants from all over the United States and Europe to celebrate the university's 20th anniversary. A doctor from Vienna, named Sigmund Freud, was to give some lectures on sex. Unfortunately, in German. Karl Jung from Switzerland was another on the list.

Then there was Emma Goldman, famed as a radical anarchist on two continents.

Miss Goldman was in town, vowing to speak on anarchism. Worcester Police Chief David Matthews vowed that she would not speak on anarchism or anything else in Worcester. Something called the Free Speech Committee materialized as if by magic. Radicals and anarchists up and down the East Coast were galvanized into action. Mayor James Logan was conveniently out of town, leaving the responsibility for Miss Goldman in the hands of Matthews. Years before, Matthews had been wounded by an arrow while fighting Indians in Arizona Territory. The Indians had finally been driven off, but Miss Goldman was not so easily dissuaded.

Emma Goldman was a name to conjure with in those days. In 1892, already known as a radical agitator, she had come to Worcester with her lover and fellow-anarchist, Alexander Berkman. They briefly ran a photography studio on Main Street and then an ice cream parlor on Providence Street. The two were waiting for the moment when the oppressed masses would rise up against the

119

capitalist monster and establish a noble, non-oppressive anarchist society. The two anarchist capitalists lived together in an apartment, scandalizing the Orthodox Jews of the Providence Street neighborhood.

The moment they were anticipating arrived on July 6, 1892, when Henry Clay Frick locked out the steelworkers at Andrew Carnegie's big plant in Homestead,

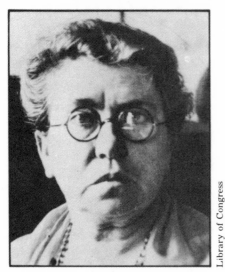
EMMA GOLDMAN

DAVID A. MATTHEWS

ALEXANDER BERKMAN

HENRY CLAY FRICK

120

Pa. When the workers rushed the gates, there was a pitched gun battle between them and the Pinkerton guards that Frick had hired. Several died on both sides.

Back in Worcester, Miss Goldman and Berkman were dizzy with excitement and fury. As anarchists in the romantic Russian tradition, they felt that the moment had come for one, tremendous, symbolic act that would galvanize the workers to revolt, toppling the rotten structure of capitalism, once and for all.

They decided that Berkman must assassinate Frick, the ultimate symbol of predatory greed.

They bought a pistol and Berkman studied how to use it. On July 23, 1892, he appeared at Frick's office in Pittsburgh. Pretending he was a strikebreaker, he gained access to the outer office and burst into Frick's inner sanctum. He pulled the trigger and hit Frick in the neck and jaw. When attendants subdued him, Frick, blood pouring down his beard, asked to see Berkman's face. For a long moment, the two men — the Russian-born anarchist and the American arch capitalist — stared into each other's eyes. It was one of the symbolic confrontations of U.S. history.

The system did not collapse. Frick is supposed to have said, as he was being taken to the hospital, "Whether I live or die, the company will prevail." He did not die and the company prevailed. Frick was a better prophet than Berkman and Miss Goldman.

Berkman got 20 years in jail, but was let out after 14, after which he resumed his career as anarchist agitator. Meanwhile Miss Goldman founded a new magazine, "Mother Earth," and became one of the most famous anarchist lecturers (some would say rabble-rousers) of her time. Controversy followed her as iron filings follow a magnet. She defended Leon Czolgoz, the assassin of President William McKinley. She endorsed sex without marriage. She smoked cigarettes in public. She condemned not only capitalism, but any reformist attempts to improve it. She thought the campaign for woman suffrage was a waste of time and effort because she thought the vote itself was a fraudulent device used by the capitalists to keep the people subservient. The only answer, she declared, was the total demolition of the capitalist system and its replacement by the principle of anarchy.

In September 1909, there she was back in Worcester, promising to declare her anarchist heresies in public. And with her, as her manager, was Dr. Ben Reitman, another noted radical. The two were carrying on what used to be called a torrid love affair.

Actually, she had come to Worcester to hear Freud, whom she had heard years before in Vienna when she was studying for her degree in nursing. His sexual theories fascinated her, although the good doctor would have been shocked at her own personal life. She believed that monogamy was part of the capitalist oppression of women, and she had many lovers besides Berkman and Reitman.

Austin P. Cristy, the crusty, hard-line Republican publisher of the Telegram, detested anarchists and radicals and everything they stood for. On the other hand, Miss Goldman was wonderful copy. The Telegram reporters, obviously fascinated with this mild-seeming but famous lady, followed her everywhere she went, taking copious notes.

"She was dressed inexpensively, wearing a light skirt of mixed scotch plaid, brown silk waist and panama hat, trimmed with brown and white plaid ribbon. Since she was in Worcester last, Miss Goldman has taken to wearing eyeglasses with extra thick lenses, which in the reverse magnify her eyes and change her whole appearance while talking," went one Telegram account.

At the Bay State House, she reminisced with a reporter.

"I walked through the streets of Worcester today and I had to marvel at the wonderful growth of the city. Everything has changed. When I was here 18 years ago, Worcester was little more than a village compared to the progressive city it looks today. I wish I could say as much about the intelligence of the police force. The police seem to have remained in the same old rut.

"They told me Worcester was no-license (no liquor sold). Why, Worcester was always no-license. When I was here first it was no-license. It is no-license on this trip. I seem to be a hoodoo for liquor, as I manage to come here when it is dry."

But she soon switched from nostalgia to the business at hand. "Worcester is the only city in Massachusetts that has tried to stop me from speaking," she said. "People have peculiar ideas about anarchists. They seem to think we go around with bombs in our pockets."

With the generous front-page coverage of the Telegram, Miss Goldman and Reitman, who said he was a member of the National Free Speech Committee, kept asking embarrassing questions of the police and the Worcester community: Given the plain words of the First Amendment, how could the police deny her the right to speak? The Telegram even published a letter from Reitman in which he expressed his views in detail.

On the third day, Mayor Logan finally showed up at his office and reluctantly granted an audience to Reitman.

The mayor was evasive. He said he could not interfere with his chief of police on a matter of public order. When Reitman asked him what he would do if the police tried to keep Miss Goldman from speaking, thus violating the First Amendment, the mayor retorted that his police "do not break the law."

The Telegram reporters, obviously enjoying the whole thing, shuttled back and forth between the Goldman-Reitman camp and the increasingly uncomfortable police chief. He now qualified his earlier edict: Although Miss Goldman would not be allowed to speak on *anarchism*, he clarified, nobody, certainly not he, ever had said that she couldn't speak on some other subject. Miss Goldman said she hadn't made up her mind as to her subject. She really couldn't say beforehand.

Meanwhile, Reitman and Miss Goldman walked the streets, attracting attention. Reitman gave a couple of impromptu speeches himself, one of them on the Common. His subject was anarchism. The Telegram reported that "Dr. Reitman, in his picturesque way, attracted much attention just by standing in one of his characteristic poses and shooting glances from between narrowed lids."

Reitman also visited Clark University and tried to meet President G. Stanley Hall. Hall was too busy to see him, what with Freud and all, but, according to the Telegram, Hall favored free speech "with limitations." What limitations he did not specify. Hall may have been irked that Reitman and Miss Goldman were getting so much front-page publicity while his 20th anniversary celebration was being reported on the inside pages.

At length, the radical duo made their move. They announced that Miss Goldman would speak Friday night at Beaver Hall on Bartlett Street (then off lower Front Street, about where the Worcester Center Galleria is now).

"ANARCHIST LEADERS ARE BOLDLY DEFIANT" trumpeted the Telegram in a front-page headline. "Should the police illegally suppress free speech at Beaver Hall, Emma Goldman will speak at the home of Rev. Eliot White, 35 Catherine Street," said Reitman.

Library of Congress

BEN REITMAN

Worcester Telegram & Gazette

JAMES LOGAN

123

The moment came. Reitman, Miss Goldman and a throng of people descended on Beaver Hall, only to find that it was locked. The custodian said he could not open the hall lest his license be revoked. So it was down Front Street, down Main Street, up Lincoln Street to Rev. White's front lawn on Catherine Street, Miss Goldman and Reitman in the lead. The Telegram likened it to a triumphal procession, with people joining the parade, everybody having a fine time.

The headline on the Telegram story the next day was:

NINETEEN COPS HEAR LECTURE ON ANARCHY

"Under the noses of 19 members of the police department and before an audience numbering about 400 persons, Emma Goldman, the anarchist leader, delivered a lecture on 'Anarchism' last night on the lawn of Rev. Eliot White's home, 35 Catherine Street, in absolute defiance of Chief of Police David A. Matthews, who yesterday repeated his avowal that Miss Goldman would not speak in Worcester with his sanction.

"It was the first dose the heart of the commonwealth has had of anarchism, and naturally the victory of the anarchists over the chief of police, raised the anarchist sympathizers and free speech enthusiasts into the seventh heaven of delight."

The Telegram went on to report in indignant detail the message that the radical lady had brought to Worcester:

"Capitalism must be done away with. Capitalism must be destroyed, whether the capitalists like it or not. Capitalism makes slaves, grinds man down until he becomes a mere machine . . . You claim to have free government in America and yet you are little better than the poor people in Russia fighting for their liberty." And much more.

The following day's Telegram story was headed:

FREE SPEECH COMMITTEE GIVES EMMA THE CASH

It said that the Worcester Free Speech Committee had turned over the proceeds of the ticket sales to Miss Goldman and then had passed three resolutions, one of which deplored the "abdication" of Mayor Logan in evading his responsibilities to uphold the Constitution and allowing the police chief to decide such an important matter.

Miss Goldman and Reitman took the 6:15 train for Providence the next night.

Chief Matthews and Mayor Logan must have breathed sighs of relief.

124

Chapter 29

The Women's Evening Gazette

ON APRIL 11, 1914, a newsworthy event occurred in Worcester. That day's edition of The Evening Gazette was reported, written, edited and laid out entirely by women.

Arabella A. Tucker was editor-in-chief, Isabelle M. Tulloch was city editor and Adah Johnson was business manager. Their staff of reporters and editors included Esther Forbes, Amy Tanner, Florence A. Bullock, Sara Southwick, Annie S. Bruninghaus, Grace MacGowan, Alice Washburn, Ellen Coombs, Vida Smith, Abbie Searle, Emma Goodwin and Alice Foster.

This was not some stuffer or extra edition to go along with the regular newspaper. This was the regular edition of the Gazette and it surely was one of the more unusual ventures in the history of journalism in Worcester, or anywhere else, for that matter. The only stylistic change on the front page was a "Woman's Club Edition" banner over the Gazette logo.

It all began with a call by Miss Tucker, president of the Worcester Woman's Club, on George F. Booth, editor and publisher of The Evening Gazette. She explained that the club was raising money to pay off the last of the mortgage on its splendid clubhouse at Wheaton Square. Would he consider letting the club-women write, edit, lay out and manage one day's edition of the Gazette as part of the fund raising?

Booth must have been astonished at the audacity of the proposal. But, having plenty of audacity himself, he soon warmed to the idea. Ground rules were set up: the Woman's Club could solicit any advertisers not under contract. Price for that edition would be five cents instead of a penny, the extra to go to the Woman's Club. Extra copies would be run off the presses to be sold as souvenirs by the women.

Twenty years later Isabelle M. Tulloch described how the women descended on the Gazette building, then at Mechanic and Norwich streets: "I can still see Billie Larkin, then the Gazette city editor, rising from his desk and offering his chair to the Woman's Club city editor for the day. It was a proud moment."

125

That edition of the Gazette is a gold mine for anyone wanting to find out what was on the minds of progressive women 70 years ago. The Worcester Woman's Club was far more than a social organization. It was the forerunner of the National Organization for Women, working hard to get women the vote and dedicated to the betterment of women, economically, politically and socially. The women who took over the Gazette on April 11, 1914, wanted to do more than just raise money; they were determined to make what we would call a feminist statement, and they succeeded brilliantly.

They made no bones about it. An editorial said, "it is so seldom that women get the ear of the public in this way, perhaps it is not strange that we have seized the occasion to exploit the work we are doing in civic life, to present some of our grievances and to give some sage advice to men, who have always been so generous to us in suggestions for the conduct of life."

Thus, the lead news story was headed: CHICAGO GIRL WILL NOT WED WORCESTER MAN. It told how Alice Young, engaged to be married to Roland F. Hall of Worcester, changed her mind at the last minute. "One Woman Exercises Prerogative" said the subhead.

FATHER'S PETITION FOR DAUGHTER IS CONTESTED BY WIFE was the head on a story from Whitinsville. Another, datelined Tallahassee, announced that FIRST WOMAN IN FLORIDA TO GET DEATH SENTENCE.

A letter to the editor urged the Worcester Police Department to appoint a woman officer "to give our girls, from homes where lies no influence for good, the protection of a woman's kindly advice . . ."

IS WOMAN PROTECTED? asked one rhetorical headline. Emma C. Marble's news story gave the answer: "Every law for the special protection of women . . . is so worded that it can be easily evaded or is wholly unenforceable." Miss Marble was particularly bitter about the 54-hour week law. "The law is unenforceable; but even if enforced it would still allow an employer to work women for excessive hours provided this alternated with occasional idle seasons." The article also pointed out that the penalty for violating the eight-hour law for men was a $1,000 fine, but only $100 for violating the 54-hour law for women.

Anna P. Smith wrote that Worcester streetcars were overcrowded, especially at rush hours, and wondered if that had anything to do with "watered stock." Grace E. Lewis warned President Woodrow Wilson not to intervene by force in Mexico lest he awaken "the devilish war spirit" in the country.

Sara Southwick wrote an article noting that the National Metal Trades Association was going to honor women for the first time. Georgie A. Bacon wrote about the upcoming biennial convention of the general federation of women's clubs in Chicago. Edith P. Kinnicutt recounted the achievements of the Worcester Branch

of the Massachusetts Civil Service Association and the continuing fight for civil service reform.

Amy Tanner wrote about the splendid work being done by a volunteer committee of the Council of Jewish Women, headed by Mrs. J.M. Talamo, in giving counseling and assistance to people discharged from Worcester City Hospital. "Why should not our City Hospital, which belongs to the people, be allowed funds for a Social Service Department?" she asked.

Dr. Amanda C. Bray's article was headed: WHY MARRIED LIFE IS SOMETIMES A FAILURE AND GETS MONOTONOUS. "Marriage," she observed, "is the one situation on earth which demands the utmost tact and we confront it with

127

a bluntness and pitiless cruelty that we would use nowhere else."

Mayor George F. Wright was interviewed. So was Mrs. Wright. She told reporter Minnie E. Wright (maybe a relation?) that billboards were getting to be a blight on the landscape and should be heavily taxed to discourage them.

The women did not neglect more traditional news items. Esther Forbes, a sports reporter who would go on to higher things, interviewed the crusty Jesse Burkett, manager of the semi-professional Worcester Climbers. "I won't say a word about woman's suffrage," he told Miss Forbes. He did say his team would be "fighting all the way" for the pennant and that "A batsman is born, not made, although we'll have to show the young fellows a lot about hitting when they break in."

Miss Forbes also interviewed Marjorie Cowee, "the first woman basketball coach of the Classical High School Aletheia. Miss Cowee, who had played four years of basketball with Classical and four years at Wellesley, said that her team, at the end of the season, "was well-balanced, and fast and machine-like."

Olive Higgins Prouty, later to achieve fame with "Stella Dallas" and other books, contributed a morality tale about a young woman brought up to think that woman's place was in the home but who eventually was persuaded to march in the Suffrage Parade.

Woman suffrage, an issue then boiling to a climax, was high on the agenda of the staff. A long discussion of the pros and cons of giving the vote to women filled almost a page. Each negative argument was systematically knocked down by a persuasive rebuttal. "American men are fairer to their women than the men of any other nation, but a man is too different by nature to be able to represent her. No matter how good his intentions, he cannot look at things from exactly her point of view."

Despite all that, the article went on, "There are branches of the Society Opposed to Further Extension of Suffrage to Women in three hundred and eighty-six cities and towns in Massachusetts with an active membership of over 23,000." The opposition seemed formidable to those progressive women of 1914.

Yet only six years later, the 19th Amendment, giving women the right to vote, became the law of the land.

The Woman's Club issue of the Gazette also included the usual women's news about recipes, church affairs and clothing styles. But Mary Trumbull sounded a rebellious note with the charge that women were the slaves of men in style, first because male clothes designers decided what the fashion would be and, second, because husbands insisted on their wives' conforming. "If you can't dress like other women, you can't expect me to be seen out with you."

Edith B. Harrington, her eye firmly on the future, wrote an article headed:

128

MANY PLEASURES OFFERED TO WOMAN WHO DRIVES HER OWN CAR.

"The gratified, satisfied feeling that a woman has who can go into her garage, get her car out herself and go when and where she chooses, without having to call for assistance, is one, that having once experienced, it will be hard to get along without," Miss Harrington wrote. It was a paean to the kind of independence that many women yearned for. She estimated that at least 100 Worcester women drove their own cars, and gave her opinion that the electric car was better suited for women than was any other kind.

It was natural, even inevitable, that a newspaper produced by members of the Worcester Woman's Club would have something to say about the club and its splendid building at Wheaton Square. Clara Lovell's piece was reasonably restrained, yet full of pride for what the club had accomplished. It included three pictures of the club building, one exterior, two interior. Miss Lovell wrote about how Josephine Wright Chapman of Boston had asked the privilege of submitting plans. Her design, competing with four other proposals, won the unanimous vote of the committee. "Naturally, the directors were proud of their sex . . ." noted Miss Lovell laconically.

The Worcester Woman's Club has done many constructive things over the past century, but few were more daring than its one-day venture into Worcester journalism. Those women of 1914 had more in common with the women of our own era than is sometimes realized.

Anyone who doubts it should take the time to look at that remarkable edition of The Evening Gazette. Nothing like it has ever been seen in this community, before or since.

OLIVE HIGGINS PROUTY

ESTHER FORBES

EX-POLICEMAN CONLIN GETS $2079.38 BACK PAY

The Evening Gazette

WORCESTER, MASS., FRIDAY, JULY 16, 1924.   "THE PAPER THAT GOES HOME"   THREE SECTIONS—TWO CENTS

30 PAGES TODAY

CYCLONE LOSS IS OVER $1,000,000;
WHALOM PARK GROVE IS IN RUINS

The picture on the left shows a giant tree uprooted in the yard of Walter M. Day on the Lunenburg road, which crashed through the barn during yesterday's cyclone. In the center is shown the portion of the house of Rector F. Coleal, in Lunenburg, which was left when the terrific wind raised the garage attached to the house to collapse, pulling the side of the house with it, exposing the pantry, which had been used only a few minutes previous for the preparation of the noonday meal. The remainder of the roof of the Parkhill Mill in Fitchburg, which was lifted completely from the top of the building and dashed down into the yard at the right of the factory.

CITY IS TO HAVE WATER TEST PLANT

Weekly Examinations to Be Possible, Due to Department Laboratory Equipped With Latest Apparatus—Most Approved Methods at Hand for War on Algae and Other Disturbers — Copper Sulphate Method Among Results of Commissioner Batchelder's New York Visit

Weather Forecast

CHARGE G. O. P. HIRED THUGS TO GAS R. I. SENATE

Affidavit in Legislative Wrangle Alleges Conspiracy by State Committee to Break Deadlock

PELKEY NAMED IN PAPER AS HIRER OF GANGSTERS

Dentist, 66, Is to Wed His Assistant, Aged 35

SMALL LOSS OF LIFE DUE TO FACT IT WAS NOON HOUR

Damaged Factories in Fitchburg Were Virtually Empty, as Workers Were at Dinner When First Tornado Recalled in Worcester County Sweeps Through Whole Northern Portion of County—Heavy Electrical Storms Do Extensive Damage All Over Central Massachusetts — Fitchburg Busy Digging Away Debris of More Than 200 Homes and Shops

MAYBE IT'S HERE!

TRUE TORNADO TYPES SEEN IN STORM'S RAGE

Clark Climatologist Says Fitchburg Visitation Phenomena Better Known West Than Here!

EFFECT OF COLD AIR WAVE IS NOT BELT

Classified Advertisers
TAKE NOTICE—

Owing to the constantly increasing circulation of The Sunday Telegram, it is necessary to start The Telegram presses earlier Sunday morning to enable us to make early morning train connections on the County Edition.

To insure insertion and proper classification in all editions of THE SUNDAY TELEGRAM, classified advertising copy must be in THE TELEGRAM office not later than 9.30 o'clock Saturday night.

THE SUNDAY TELEGRAM is now printing and distributing more than 58,000 copies every Sunday.

Write your copy and bring it or send it to THE TELEGRAM office early.

56 ELIGIBLES FOR FIRE DEPARTMENT

Names of Men Who Passed Examinations Are Filed at City Hall

President Eliot's Wife Dies in Maine

G. F. REDMOND CONVICTED BY FEDERAL JURY

Court at Boston Defers Sentence for Conspiracy and Mail Fraud Pending Motions Seeking Appeal

T. J. CONLIN, JR., TO GET $2079.38

Commissioner Dana Forfeits One-Fourth Pay of Former Worcester Policeman

PROTECTIVE UNION TO HAVE NEW HOME

Holy Cross Faculty Changes Announced

Worcester Weather

Car Routes Changed During Track Repairs

Chapter 30

When the Twister Struck Fitchburg

JULY 17, 1924, was a hot sultry day in Fitchburg. When the noon whistle blew, hundreds of workers poured out of the big Parkhill Mills factory and the Grant Yarn Co. next door, seeking a fresh breeze while they walked home for lunch. Little did they know that they had escaped death by minutes.

At about 12:17, a sullen roar was heard to the west. Gusts of wind seemed to explode out of the black, boiling sky. Lightning flashed and people ran for cover. Then came something that no one had ever seen before — a windstorm of fury and destruction.

For the next 12 minutes, Fitchburg was in the grip of a tornado, the only one in its history.

The roof of the Parkhill Mill No. 3, more than 200 feet long, was stripped from the big factory building as if it had been an orange peel. Tons of debris filled the cavernous building where, minutes before, hundreds of people had been working at their benches and machines. A heavy electric motor that powered the plant's fourth floor was hurled 75 feet through the factory wall and plunged through the roof of an adjoining building. One side of the Grant mill collapsed into rubble.

A 50-foot-tall chimney on the Dejonge Paper Co. mill came crashing down, killing Matthew Dzingas instantly. Dozens of roofs were torn off houses, some never to be seen again in recognizable form. Automobiles were tossed into the air like toys. Hundreds of great trees were uprooted and splintered like matchwood. So many power and telephone lines were down that Fitchburg was isolated from the outside world for hours.

Downtown Fitchburg escaped the main explosive force of the storm, possibly because it is located in a valley. But the Cleghorn district was wrecked. Houses there were flattened, unroofed, tipped over, lifted off their foundations and dropped, twisted and grotesque. Chimneys were leveled as if by a mammoth scythe. Bricks, boards, furniture, shingles, broken glass, window blinds were scattered everywhere.

131

There were the usual freakish anomalies. Patrick Terrault's garage, containing four cars, was moved 60 feet. The cars were undamaged. Frank Allen's fireworks store, complete with stock, was blown into the Nashua River and washed away. William Winslow's roof was lifted off his house at 2 Harvard St. and dumped on Richard Weston's roof across the road. Mrs. Natalie Leonard of River Street was left with only one bedroom and a bathroom standing.

While the people of Fitchburg were still staring with shock at the devastation, the tornado was demolishing Whalom Park. Hundreds of beautiful pine trees were torn up by the roots. Every small building in the park was flattened and strewn about. Cottages on the shore were swept away in the gale. The YMCA tent camp was obliterated.

Robert and Paul Alexander of Leominster had a bizarre experience. They were out on the lake in a boat when the destruction began. Friends on shore called to them to lie flat in the bottom of the boat, which was then whipped at tremendous speed the length of the lake before it capsized 75 feet from shore on the Lunenburg side. They were able to make it to shore.

Edward Laventure, 13, was not so lucky. He drowned in the roiling waters when the wind upturned his canoe.

The twister — possibly more than one — moved on. It, or another one, had done considerable damage in South Gardner. In Westminster, it snapped the top 15 feet off the Universalist Church steeple, but left the church otherwise intact. Violent winds blew down trees and telephone poles in Leominster, but Leominster was spared the teeth of the deadly twister. Winds and thunderstorms were reported from many places that day, from Westboro to Lowell.

Although the Fitchburg tornado damaged or destroyed more than 200 buildings and did more than $1 million damage to property, amazingly it caused only two deaths. About 25 people were injured seriously enough to be treated at hospitals. Had the storm struck 25 minutes earlier, the toll might have been in the hundreds.

The tornado or "cyclone" was the talk of the county for weeks. Dr. Charles Brooks, professor of meteorology at Clark University, explained that the Fitchburg tornado was a rare phenomenon in which "the atmospheric disturbance is so great, the convulsion so intense, that a rotary motion is imparted to the air, rapidly becoming more intense, and a vortex forms, first in the clouds and then reaching down until it touches the ground.

"The funnel travels rapidly across the country. Its great force, however, is in the terrific speed of the air as it swirls about in a spiral, faster by far than any gale."

For a time Fitchburg people claimed distinction as the only place in Massachusetts ever to be hit by a tornado. But then some with long memories recalled that a tornado had hit Lawrence on July 27, 1890, killing eight and doing much damage. Others looked back even farther, to the twister that tore through the center of Holden in June, 1871.

The Fitchburg tornado was not the first to ravage Central Massachusetts, nor would it be the last.

Worcester Telegram & Gazette Photos

By June 1953, the Fitchburg tornado had been mostly forgotten except by those who lived through it. But it still ranks as the second most violent tornado ever to strike Worcester County.

133

Facsimile of the front page of the *Sunday Telegram*, Worcester, Mass., Sunday Morning, October 19, 1924, with the headline "KLANSMEN BEATEN IN STREET, CARS STONED, WOMEN INJURED."

134

Chapter 31

Worcester's Klans and Kleagles

*T*HE KU KLUX KLAN probably burned its first cross in Worcester County some time in 1922, although no one knows for sure.

In the three years following, it spread across Central Massachusetts like a brush fire in drought time. Secret KKK meetings and public "Klonvocations" were held in Marlboro, West Brookfield, Millbury, Holden, Stow, Berlin, Charlton, Lancaster, Shrewbury, Upton, Paxton and other nearby communities. As the crosses flamed on rural hills, the meetings and counter-demonstrations grew ugly. Sporadic fighting turned into near riots. Police were called out to break up angry crowds. A news reporter covering a Klan meeting in Blackstone was "branded" on the forehead with a "K."

In most parts of the country, the Klan was a rural and small town phenomenon. In Central Massachusetts, Worcester was the focal point of Klan activity for the entire region. In September 1923, a huge Klan rally filled both Mechanics Hall and Washburn Hall and attracted thousands of onlookers who jammed Main and Walnut streets for blocks. A year later, an even larger "Klonvocation" was held at the Fairgrounds on West Boylston Street. That rally turned into fist fights, beatings, stonings of cars and general rioting. Heads were bloodied and police reserves called out.

This bizarre chapter in our local history has faded away. Those old enough to remember have forgotten — sometimes conveniently. Those too young to remember can hardly imagine that Worcester once was called the "Klan capital" of Massachusetts — or why. Not one Worcester school student in a thousand is remotely aware of what was going on here and throughout New England in the 1920s.

Why Worcester? Why New England? As the saying goes, it was part of a larger picture.

The original Ku Klux Klan was born in the South after the Civil War and soon became the chief enforcer of white supremacy in the region. By beatings, lynchings, threats and other atrocities it drove southern blacks out of politics and kept

135

them in a segregated, second-rate status that was to endure for a century. Although most southern whites approved of segregation, the excesses of the Klan led the federal and state governments to outlaw it in the 1870s. It gradually withered away.

The second Ku Klux Klan was organized in 1915 at Stone Mountain, Ga., by William Joseph Simmons, its first "Imperial Wizard." That also was the year that D.W. Griffith released his famous motion picture, "The Birth of a Nation," which glorified the old Klan and caused riots and lynchings in some parts of the South.

Simmons was basically a romantic who had heard stirring tales about the original KKK from his grandfather. He dreamed of a national Klan dedicated to the principles of "true Americanism." That was the code phrase for white, Anglo-Saxon Protestantism.

The revived Klan gradually found fertile soil in an country faced with a flood of immigrants, many of whom were Catholic and Jewish. The social shock of World War I and its aftermath added fuel to the fire. In the minds of many small-town folk, the Ku Klux Klan, whatever its origins, seemed to stand for patriotism, Americanism, tradition. and "Christianity." A congressional investigation of the Klan in 1921 gave it nationwide publicity and led to a huge influx of new members.

Enter Hiram Wesley Evans, a born organizer and promoter. He bought out Simmons' copyrights to the Klan for $146,000, revamped the top administration and began to spread the Klan virus from the Atlantic to the Pacific.

Evans was shrewd. He saw that there was big money to be made from the KKK. Membership in the Klan cost $10. This "Klecktoken" was split three ways — $4 to the recruiter, $6 to regional headquarters, where the King Kleagle of the region took $1 and the Grand Goblin 50 cents. The other $4.50 was supposed to be sent to national KKK headquarters, but there was a lot of leakage. From first to last, the KKK was plagued by enormous embezzlements. It was an odd combination of hucksterism, nativism, opportunism and perverted idealism. Many gullible people joined the Klan in the belief that it stood for high moral principles and "Americanism."

The Klan spread — how it spread! At its peak it may have numbered five million members. It was a political power in a dozen states, strong enough to control state elections in some. Grand Goblin David C. Stephenson was the virtual dictator of Indiana. The KKK was strong in the South and in parts of the Midwest and the North, including northern New England.

People in Maine, New Hampshire and Vermont embraced the Klan because they resented the influx of French Canadians who took jobs at low wages. In Massachusetts and Rhode Island, the Klan battened on yet another revival of the

136

ancient animosity toward the Irish and other "foreign" Catholics. In Connecticut, Rhode Island and eastern Massachusetts, anti-Italian feeling played a part, possibly stimulated by the Sacco-Vanzetti case. Variations on the prejudice theme were played across the country.

The first organizer of the Klan in Massachusetts was A.J. Padon, a kleagle from Indiana. He and a half-dozen henchmen began setting up "klaverns" around Boston in 1921. In 1922 they reached Worcester, where they found receptive souls in the British-American Orange lodges, traditionally anti-Irish and anti-Catholic. The first Klan leaders in the city were Clarence J. Kearney and Bertram B. Priest, both members of the Orange lodge.

Kearney and Priest signed up a couple of hundred members here. But it took a man from Maine, King Kleagle R. Eugene Farnsworth, to really set Worcester on fire. Farnsworth was the main speaker at the enormous KKK rally at Mechanics Hall on Sept. 27, 1923. It was a traumatic experience for the city.

For weeks beforehand the issue was how to stop the meeting. Mayor Peter F. "Fish" Sullivan was under pressure from several directions to see that the event was canceled. The City Council denounced the Klan by a vote of 26-1. Most city ministers attacked it, although a few favored the Klan. The Masons were particularly insistent that the Klan not be permitted to assemble in Worcester. But Sullivan had no power to cancel a meeting for which a lawful permit had been granted.

A few days before the scheduled event, the Worcester Evening Post printed a verse by Katherine H. Cronin on its front page in large type. One stanza gives the flavor:

> "When Mechanics Hall was founded and its cornerstone was placed,
> Elbridge Boyden's architecture that has never been disgraced;
> Offspring of the love and labor of a true American —
> Do you think they planned the platform for the lawless
> Ku Klux Klan?"

Mayor Sullivan was in a box. Two days before the scheduled meeting, he wrote a plea to the Worcester County Mechanics Association, asking the officers to cancel the permit issued to the Klan "to preserve order and prevent any possible disturbance." The assocation, founded 80 years before to promote free discussion, found the ball in its corner.

After a long debate behind closed doors, the hall committee respectfully declined the mayor's request. "The hall," they wrote him, "for many years has been an open forum for any meeting or discussion and we do not feel that this policy should be changed . . ."

There's no denying that the committee — Edward J. Cross, Alanson Robbins and Charles Cather — showed courage.

And so the dreaded event took place as planned. One hundred police were on duty, and another 100 held in readiness. Capt. Thomas F. Foley, later chief, was in charge of the police detail. An appeal by the mayor to "all good Worcester people" to stay away fell on deaf ears. Mechanics Hall and Washburn Hall were filled to overflowing, while an estimated 5,000 milled about on Main Street.

Mechanics Hall never had a livelier night in all its long history. The crowd in Washburn Hall listened to J.E. Stout, a kleagle from Detroit. Upstairs in the great hall, Farnsworth put on a star performance, strutting about the stage, making caustic remarks about the newsmen on hand and newspapers in general, quipping about the "lies" that were told about the KKK and introducing a singing group.

The Klan, he said, was not against any race or group. But it was for unadulterated, "unhyphenated" Americanism, and for the public school system, and for Prohibition. He made insinuating remarks against Jews, Italians and "foreigners" — remarks that were loudly appreciated by the audience.

Farnsworth, a native of Fitchburg and a former drummer for the Salvation Army, probably hit the peak of his Klan career that night. But, since he had been assigned the territory of northern New England — Maine, New Hampshire and Vermont — he was invading the territory of another kleagle. A few months later, in one of the many internal disputes that split the Klan leadership periodically, he was ousted.

The Mechanics Hall Klan rally brought in an avalanche of new members — perhaps 1,500 to 2,000, according to one estimate. It opened the eyes of the Boston kleagles to something interesting: Worcester's large Swedish population was prime territory for Klan missionary work.

The membership lists tell the story. Of the almost 5,000 Klan members in Worcester in 1925 (including about 900 "Kamelias" who belonged to the women's auxiliary) 40 percent had Swedish names. In 1924, unbeknownst to the national Klan headquarters, Worcester Klan recruiters began to use a special membership form. Question 7 was changed from "Were your parents born in the United States of America?" to "Are you a Nordic American?" There was Leif Ericsson Klavern in Greendale and other klaverns on Bell Hill and in Quinsigamond Village.

Thus, in Worcester, this supposedly 100 percent American organization, dedicated to restricted immigration, included many who had been born abroad.

However, the bulk of the Klan in Worcester as elsewhere was composed of native-born Americans. The Klan appealed to many groups and many walks of life.

The year 1924 saw the Klan at its height in Worcester County and probably across the country. That was the year of the famous deadlocked Democratic National Convention, when Al Smith and William G. McAdoo battled for 103 votes before the exhausted convention turned to John W. Davis for its presidential candidate.

Smith's candidacy sharpened the issue of Catholicism and stimulated the Klan's political activities. When pro-Smith forces introduced an anti-Klan plank at the 1924 convention, the delegates split right down the middle. Old William Jennings Bryan, representing the "dry" Protestant states of the Midwest and South, pleaded before the platform committee for compromise. "Just remove three words — that's all we ask," he pleaded. But the convention remained hopelessly divided between the big-city, Catholic-Jewish wing of the party, and the rural, Protestant Democrats of the South and Midwest.

In Worcester County, the Klan seemed unstoppable in 1924. A chronology compiled by Professor Vincent E. Powers shows what was happening by mid-summer.

July 2 — Riot at KKK meeting in Stow.
July 8 — Klan meetings in several towns.
July 11 — Klan rally in Westboro.
July 22 — Riot barely averted at KKK meeting in Berlin.
July 24 — Cross burned before Catholic church in Charlton.
July 29 — Riot at Lancaster KKK meeting leading to gunfire.
         A smaller riot in Spencer.
July 30 — Gov. Cox urges an end to Klan violence.
July 31 — Police disarm KKK in Shrewsbury.
Aug. 2 — Klan trying to enlist Worcester city police.
Aug. 3 — Grafton minister announces he is a Kluxer.
Aug. 4 — Klan to initiate 500 in Worcester this week.
Aug. 5 — State police pour into central Massachusetts to keep the
         peace.
Aug. 7 — City KKK to go to big Klonvocation in New Hampshire.
Aug. 13 — Klan meeting in Shrewsbury.
Aug. 20 — Klan meeting in Berlin.
Aug. 22 — Klan meetings in Stow and Upton.
Aug. 23, 24, 25 — Klan meetings in Upton.
Aug. 27 — Klan meeting in Paxton.
Aug. 29 — Klan meeting in Shrewsbury.
Aug. 30 — Klan meeting in Stow.

Things were getting tense. The meetings were becoming more ugly as anti-Klan groups began to form. In Rutland and Millbury, Klansmen were stoned. Crosses were burned in Worcester on Newton Hill, Belmont Hill and in front of Notre Dame convent on Plantation Street.

The Worcester Klan became outspoken on local issues. It accused city politicians of being in league with bootleggers; it opposed an Italo-American proposal to rename Shrewsbury Street "Columbus Avenue," and it denounced the "high life" in colleges. The Klan also called for nonpartisan city elections — something that was adopted years later when the Klan had long since faded away.

James Michael Curley was running for governor. As mayor of Boston he had kept the Klan at bay by bluntly using the licensing power. Any hall owner in Boston who rented to the Klan could expect a quick and thorough inspection that would close him down indefinitely.

Curley used the Klan for his own political purposes. At more than one of his rallies he had a cross burned as a prelude to a moving oration:

"There it burns, the cross of hatred upon which our Lord, Jesus Christ, was crucified — the cross of human avarice and not the cross of love and charity."

It always brought down the house, as the saying goes, but Curley still lost the election to Alvan Fuller, who kept reminding the voters that Mrs. Fuller was a Catholic.

As autumn wore on, rumors of a giant Klonvocation to be held at the Fairground began to sweep the county. Demands rose again that the Klan be blocked. Francis P. McKeon, campaigning for mayor, said that the Klan would never dare show its head in Worcester if he were manning the ramparts at City Hall.

However, since the Mechanics Hall rally the previous year had gone off without any major trouble, Mayor Michael J. O'Hara did not try very hard to stop the Fairgrounds Klonvocation.

It was probably the largest KKK gathering ever held in New England. An estimated 15,000 people attended the all-day affair on Oct. 19. At least 1,000 Klansmen were on hand, fully garbed in sheets and hoods. For most of the day, things went smoothly.

Newspaper accounts differ on just what happened. The riot started with the stoning of a few cars. Windows were broken. Then fighting broke out all the way from the Fairgrounds to Harrington Corner. A huge and hostile mob, numbering in the thousands, surrounded the Fairgrounds and caused the King Kleagle to appeal to the Worcester Police for protection. Klan members and spectators leaving the meeting were beaten up and threatened. Some cars were smashed. A biplane with a large "KKK" sign painted on its fuselage was forced to land near Burncoat Street, setting off rumors that it had been shot down. The pilot denied that story and took off. But the story spread around the country and is related as fact in David M. Chalmers' "Hooded America," one of the best studies of the KKK.

That was the high-water mark for the Klan in Worcester. After that, membership began to fall off. Klan meetings were not as well attended, and Klan membership no longer was flaunted. Boycotts became a serious problem for Klan-owned businesses. To stay in business, the owners of Town Talk Bakery and other enterprises had to publicly deny they were Klan members.

Furthermore, a series of sex and money scandals at the national level revealed the Klan for what it really was.

Although anti-Catholic feeling still was strong in some places in 1928, when Al Smith won the Democratic nomination and ran against Herbert Hoover, the Klan already was in a steep decline. By the 1930s and the Great Depression, it was little more than a bad dream in this part of the country.

Questions remain. Why did this agent of bigotry appeal to so many solid, middle-classd Americans? Why did this ugly remnant of lynch days in the old South so inflame the hearts and minds of ordinary middle-class people in Worcester County, Mass.?

What kind of person was attracted by the Klan message? What kind of person actually joined the Klan? Robert Duffus, who studied the Klan in the 1920s, listed six main categories:

1. *Professional organizers and promoters out to make a quick buck.*
2. *Businessmen and shopkeepers who feared Klan boycotts or who hoped that Klan patronage would be good for business.*
3. *Politicians who felt that Klan support would help their candidacies.*
4. *Thrill seekers and "joiners."*
5. *Criminals, particularly bootleggers, who felt they needed Klan protection.*
6. *Average persons, including some ministers, who were concerned about the decline of patriotism, religion, tradition, etc., and who saw a menace in "foreign" institutions and ideas.*

Most of those who joined the Klan in Worcester County probably fell into the last category. Many were sincere in their beliefs, and unaware of the corruption and cynical manipulations of the Klan organizers at the regional and national levels.

Yet, even when all the explanations are made, it still seems bizarre that the Ku Klux Klan should have captured the hearts and minds of thousands here in Worcester County. The area had few blacks. The KKK won no support from the political and business leaders of the community, it was condemned by all major Worcester newspapers, it was denounced by most established churches and ministers, and it had an ugly tradition to live down. Perhaps only those who were caught up in it at the time can explain why.

Unfortunately most of those first-hand witnesses are no longer around. The few who are still with us probably have long since chosen to forget their participation in this dark episode.

Robert Wilson

A typical scene at the Grafton Airport in its heyday.

Robert Wilson

The Grafton Airport in 1938. The "runways" are faintly visible.

142

Chapter 32

When Worcester Took to the Skies

THE DEDICATION of the Worcester Airport was a day to remember. More than 30,000 people showed up. The roads leading to the airport were jammed for miles with cars.

The crowd gasped at the daring stunt flyers and parachuter. Marine pilots showed off the newest military planes. A woman pilot from Germany did daring maneuvers. City and state dignitaries orated and got their pictures taken.

It all happened on Oct. 12, 1927 — in North Grafton. That was where Worcester soared into the air age that the Wright brothers had launched 24 years before.

Brigham Hill — once the George B. Inches farm — today is mostly covered with houses. But 50 years ago, it was known as Whittall Field, a place where James P. and Whitin Whittall flew canvas-covered biplanes in the years after World War I.

For the Whittall brothers and their contemporaries, flying was mostly an adventure. But when the U.S. government began shipping the mail by air, and when the larger cities began to lay out airports for future passenger service, people began to see that even smaller cities like Worcester were going to need airports. As early as 1925, an informal committee of Worcester businessmen and flying enthusiasts was set up to look at plausible sites. The two prime locations were Brigham Hill and the Eaton Field in Auburn.

Whitin Whittall, irked at the slow pace of the committee, took matters into his own hands. He got an engineer to submit rough layouts of runways for both fields and decided that the North Grafton site was the better. He signed options on the land and then talked to influential people like George Booth, editor and publisher of the Telegram and Gazette, John White, president of Worcester Bank and Trust, and George Jeppson, president of Norton Co. At a meeting held at the Worcester Club, James Whittall convinced a group of Worcester's movers and shakers that the city must have an airport and that North Grafton was the right place for it. A fund-raising committee was set up, chaired by Matthew P. Whittall. It raised $50,000 in three weeks and Worcester Airport Incorporated was set

143

up with George Jeppson as president. By Oct. 3, 1927, a 2,000-foot runway, an 1,800-foot runway and two hangars were ready for business.

And that was the only airport that Worcester had until 1945. For those 18 years, it was a busy place. Wiley Post landed there. So did Clarence Chamberlain and Ruth Nichols, early flight pioneers. Jose Iturbi flew in for a recital in Worcester. Frank Hawks, holder of many early speed records, cracked up his plane when he failed to clear a stone wall at the edge of the field and spent weeks in the hospital. Joseph Ruseckas, a flight instructor, still remembers how busy the field was in the years before World War II with the Civil Pilots Training (CPT) program.

An exciting moment at Grafton came in 1945, when the heavy drone of a four-engined plane was heard from the direction of Lake Quinsigamond. A B-17, flaps down, was coming in for a landing. As people stared in disbelief, the 30-ton bomber settled heavily onto the short strip, churning up loam and turf as it braked to a stop. The pilot, a 19-year-old lieutenant, had become disoriented. Low on fuel, he decided to land at Grafton.

Getting the big plane off was even more hair-raising. Ninety truckloads of gravel were brought in to fill the ruts the plane had made. With every ounce of extra weight removed and with only enough gasoline to get to Bradley Field, the bomber rolled down the field, engines roaring at full throttle. When it hit a bump at the end of the runway, it bounced into the air and slowly gained enough altitude to miss the trees.

But that was the only four-engined plane ever to land at Grafton. By 1940, Worcester had become the largest city in the country without regular passenger air service.

World War II, with its huge development of airpower and air transport, forced Worcester to take another look at the coming age of flight. As early as 1931, a study committee had concluded that North Grafton did not offer enough room for expansion and that Worcester should consider developing the old Battery B field on Tatnuck Hill as a modern airport. In 1940, urged by a number of prominent people, Mayor William Bennett contacted state and federal military authorities and found that the property would be available for an airport if the city wanted it. Bennett then tried to get the Board of Aldermen and the City Council to approve the transfer of $200 for a feasibility study. But a die-hard group of aldermen fought the idea, tooth and nail. The Labor News, published by Freeman Saltus, blasted the whole idea. If Worcester fell for this nonsense, Saltus wrote, it might end up spending $200,000. And for what? Who needed an airport anyway?

All during the summer and fall, the mayor tried to get the $200 approved, but was unsuccessful. It was a classic example of the kind of obstructionist politics that the city had to contend with in the old days.

Finally, in frustration, private individuals raised $1,100 for a study of the airport by Capt. Leroy Odell and Robert Aldrich. They found the site eminently feasible for a number of reasons. The land was relatively isolated from heavy residential development, it offered room for expansion, and the city's Water Department already owned the adjoining property.

But there was still disagreement between those who favored expanding the North Grafton airport and those who favored Battery B. One of those dubious about the Battery B location was Robert W. Stoddard, a flyer of long experience. He pointed out that the top of the hill, 1,000 feet above sea level, would be socked in by fog a lot more than the Grafton site, 500 feet lower. Although Stoddard eventually came around to thinking that, all things considered, the Tatnuck site was more satisfactory, bad weather has been a problem at the Worcester Airport.

Despite the doubters, the Odell study settled the matter. A bond issue was floated and construction started in 1944. The field was dedicated on May 4, 1946, when a plane carrying dignitaries from Boston landed at Worcester. On May 10, 1946, Northeast Airlines started service to New York City with several round trips a day. Mohawk Airlines started service to Albany, Rochester and Buffalo in 1953. Since then, the Worcester Airport has had good years and bad. In June, 1985, Piedmont Airlines began jet service twice a day between Worcester and the Baltimore/Washington International Airport. Once again, the skies seemed to be clearing.

And North Grafton? The Jennings brothers, Mason and Perry, ran the field until 1951. But fewer and fewer planes used it toward the end. Finally it was closed down, sold and developed for houses. Today there is little trace of the Jennies, Robins, Wacos, Fords, Stearmans, Cubs, Taylorcraft and autogiros that so fascinated the huge crowds that day so many years ago.

Occasionally, someone will comment that Worcester made a mistake when it went to Battery B instead of expanding Whittall Field. No doubt, North Grafton's weather is better for flying.

But what would North Grafton be like today with big jets using a 7,000 or 8,000-foot runway? One thing is for sure: It wouldn't have as many houses and people.

145

MARGARET SANGER

MIN CHIU CHANG

GREGORY PINCUS

Worcester Telegram & Gazette Photos

146

Chapter 33

The Big Fight Over Birth Control

THE CONTROVERSY over abortion has a familiar ring to Massachusetts residents over 40. Some of the arguments, some of the passion, even some of the actors were part of an equally bitter struggle over birth control in this state a generation ago. The controversy eventually was solved through the political process in a reasonable way.

The modern generation may find it hard to believe, but the sale and purchase of contraceptives were illegal in Massachusetts until 1966. The law was changed in that year after the U.S. Supreme Court ruled in Griswold vs. Connecticut that birth control was legal for married couples. Before that, Massachusetts doctors could not legally give contraceptive information even to *married* people, let alone single women. Doctors occasionally were prosecuted for doing just that. Their arguments that they were trying to protect the health and even the lives of women fell on deaf ears.

Despite the law, birth control was as widespread in Massachusetts at that time as in any other state. Contraceptives were sold in every drugstore, thanks to an ingenious court case of many years back. In that instance, a man was brought into court on the charge that he had purchased a contraceptive. But after his lawyer argued that there was no proof that his client had actually *used* the device, he was acquitted. Massachusetts residents made do for years under that bit of legal hypocrisy.

But the plight of poor women with large families was becoming a charged social issue. Many states quietly rewrote their laws governing contraception. By the 1930s, Massachusetts and Connecticut were the only two states with Comstock-style laws on the books. Elsewhere, doctors could legally give contraceptive advice to married women. Birth control clinics became widespread.

In 1932, the Birth Control League of Massachusetts (later the Planned Parenthood League) opened a clinic in Brookline to give advice to poverty-stricken married women referred to them for health reasons by social agencies. It was called the Mother's Health Office. By 1937, there were seven such clinics in the

147

state, one of them in Worcester. In 1937, three of them were raided, staffs were arrested and confidential records seized. Overnight, birth control became a political issue. It was to roil Massachusetts politics for the next 30 years, during which the Democrats came to dominate the state while the Republicans steadily withered away.

The birth control issue had been building up ever since Margaret Sanger, before World War I, began her long, passionate and ultimately triumphant crusade to make contraception legal. Although her own lifestyle seemed to support the notion that birth control led to "immorality," as her critics charged (among her string of lovers were H.G. Wells and Havelock Ellis), no one could match her as a publicist and polemicist. When the Massachusetts Planned Parenthood League invited her to come to the state to speak for the cause, she jumped at the chance.

To endorse birth control in those days was to cross swords with the Roman Catholic Church. In 1930, after the Anglican Church cautiously endorsed birth control for married couples, Pope Pius X issued an encyclical, *Casti Connubi*. It stated the church's position on contraception in unmistakable terms: The only permissible forms of birth control are abstinence or the rhythm method. That teaching has never changed.

Mrs. Sanger, the former Maggie Higgins, loved to battle with her ancestral church. She asserted that abstinence was "positively harmful to health." She moved through Massachusetts like a triumphant revivalist, preaching the good word to large throngs. More than 1,600 jammed Community Church in Boston to hear her fiery talk. She was enthusiastically applauded in Hyannis and Worcester.

Then came Holyoke, and Msgr. John F. Fagan of St. Jerome's, the mother Catholic church of that city. Mrs. Sanger was scheduled to speak at the First Congregational Church. A prominent member of that church was also the president of the Holyoke National Bank. When Msgr. Fagan called him and indicated that Catholics might withdraw their funds from the bank, the Congregational Church withdrew its invitation to Mrs. Sanger. She finally spoke in a tiny union hall but to a nationwide audience, thanks to the intensive news coverage.

Although Msgr. Fagan won the battle, he helped lose the war. Birth control was one thing; free speech was another. Miss Sanger's Holyoke visit won her more publicity than all the others put together. Msgr. Fagan's hardball tactics raised the old fears about the Catholic church's role in a democratic society.

In 1942, after being rebuffed by the Massachusetts Legislature, the birth control proponents gathered signatures and put a referendum question on the ballot. It would have allowed doctors to give contraceptive advice to married women in cases where health was a factor. The Catholic Church was opposed. The referendum was soundly defeated.

In 1948, after six more years of rancorous argument, a second referendum went on the ballot. The Catholic church was still opposed, but most Protestants and most Jews were in favor. Rev. Angus Dun, dean of the Episcopal Theological School in Cambridge, went on the radio to denouce the antis. "Public statements are being made, announcing that to vote 'Yes' is to favor the sale of contraceptives on the open counters of drug stores and barber shops and to encourage unlawful sex relations between boys and girls . . . Those who spread such statements are the public purveyors of lies and do not know the first principles of honorable debate." That was rough stuff.

The 1948 referendum lost, but by a narrower margin than six years before. In the 1948 campaign, many Catholic doctors were conspicuously silent. An unknown number of Catholics voted yes, in anonymous defiance of their bishops. In 1943, Fortune published a poll showing that 69 percent of Catholic women felt that contraceptive information should be made available to married couples.

The 1948 referendum was a watershed, although it didn't seem so at the time. Even though 18 more years were to go by before Massachusetts updated its birth control laws (ironically, written generations before by fundamentalist Protestants), the old statutes gradually became a dead issue as far as people's lives were concerned. They were increasingly ignored by doctors and laypersons alike.

By the time of John F. Kennedy's bid for the presidency, winds of change were blowing through the Catholic Church, from the Vatican on down. There was more concern about uncontrolled birth rates. Terms like the "population explosion" and the "population bomb" became fashionable. There was hopeful talk about a change in the Vatican's position.

Then, while Kennedy was campaigning for the presidency, out of the blue came an incredible Catholic political blunder. At about the same time that Kennedy was telling the Texas Baptist Convention that he believed in a strict separation of church and state, and that clergymen should stay out of politics, the Roman Catholic bishops of Puerto Rico issued a pastoral letter denying the sacraments to any Catholic who voted for the Popular Democratic Party led by Luis Munoz Marin. Marin's sin was his unwillingness to repeal an old law that permitted the distribution of birth control literature. The Kennedy campaign team was aghast. So was the Vatican. The bishops were summarily assigned to less prestigious posts.

Marin was re-elected by an overwhelming margin. Kennedy was elected by a razor-thin margin. Had he been defeated, part of the blame would have gone to those Puerto Rican bishops.

By the 1960s, many priests and even some of the Catholic hierarchy began to

149

realize that birth control was a no-win issue for the church. Married Catholics just did not agree with the Vatican's teaching. When a bill was introduced into the Massachusetts Legislature in 1965 for a change in the law, Archbishop Richard Cushing said he had no objection. He said it would be improper for his church to force its views on a pluralistic society.

Nonetheless, the Legislature still voted that bill down. Old habits are hard to change. It was not until 1966 that Gov. John Volpe signed a bill that finally retired the old Comstock law, after 118 years of service. From then on, it was legal for doctors to advise married people about contraception and legal for vendors to distribute contraceptive devices.

Paradoxes abound in this odd story of sex, religion and politics. One of them is that, when Margaret Sanger convinced Katherine McCormick in 1950 to put up money to develop a birth control method, she came to the Worcester Foundation for Experimental Biology, right in the heart of anti-birth control country. (Drs. John Rock, Min chiu Chang and Gregory Pincus prudently did their research in Puerto Rico, not Massachusetts).

Another paradox came when Mrs. Sanger, late in life, visited Japan. When she was told that more than a million abortions were performed every year on Japanese women, she trembled in indignation. Abortion, she proclaimed, was a barbarous outrage. It sapped the strength of mothers. Far better to prevent conception, she said, than to interrupt a pregnancy.

The birth control controversy is over and done with. The once intractable arguments, the pickets, the passion, the signs and the threats have been dissolved in the political process. People in Massachusetts and elsewhere finally concluded that it is futile to try to impose a particular moral point of view on a pluralistic, democratic society when a majority does not agree with it.

Chapter 34

The Storm That Flattened New England

THOUSANDS OF PEOPLE IN PETERSHAM, Rutland, Holden, Worcester, Shrewsbury and Westboro still have nerve-chilling memories of the killer tornado of June, 1953. They remember the black, boiling clouds, the ungodly screech of the wind, the automobiles and buses tumbled about like toys, and the screams of the injured and dying.

But thousands of other fortunate people, like me, had no idea of what was happening a few miles away. I was in Leicester clearing brush that sultry afternoon. The tornado was gone before I even heard about it.

Not so with the other great New England weather catastrophe of the last half century. The hurricane of September 1938 struck a whole region, from Long Island Sound to northern Maine. It cut a path 100 miles wide. Persons who were in it or anywhere near it will never forget the experience. Hurricane Gloria, which knocked down some trees and powerlines in late September 1985, was a mild breeze by comparison.

I was at our farm in Leicester on that awesome afternoon. Here are some of the impressions that stay with me yet:

My father, peering at the old ship's barometer that hung in our hallway and saying in a bemused voice that he had never seen the mercury fall so low. There was an eerie calm in the air. He wondered what it meant.

The first howling blast that struck from the southeast, blowing out most of the windows on that side of the farmhouse and plastering the living room with green leaves, stripped off the maple trees outside. The plaster and wallpaper were stained with green splotches. We never were able to wash off those green stains. The ceilings had to be repainted and the wallpaper replaced.

Our running out toward the barn in the blinding sheets of rain while my father shouted "Close the doors! Close the doors! Save the roof!" He feared that the wind would blast in through the big barn doors and lift the roof right off. In the nick of time we rolled the big doors shut and held them fast with large stones rolled against them.

151

The September 1938 hurricane was vastly more destructive than Hurricane Gloria in September, 1985. Many miles of railroad lines were undermined, millions of trees were destroyed and beautiful parks were strewn with splintered tree limbs and trash. The scars on the landscape remained visible for years.

152

Our trying to save the windmill that pumped the water to the tank in the attic. With the tower creaking and the wheel spinning crazily, my brother climbed the steel ladder and attached a rope to the top platform. But it was in vain; in a few minutes, the windmill tower came crashing down, a tangle of angle iron. The wheel was bent like a pretzel.

Boards, tree limbs and debris flying through the air, driven by a wind of more than 100 mph. The squawking hens were scattered like milkweed seeds on the gale. I think some of them vanished forever.

The frightening roar, like an artillery barrage, as a tall stand of pines next to our orchard was leveled into a tortured maze of stumps, upturned roots and splintered logs.

Our usually placid pond, where an angry churn of muddy water covered the whole dam, making a waterfall 40 feet wide. Miraculously the dam survived.

The muscle-straining effort required to walk in the face of that screeching wind, the rain driving like pellets of glass into our faces.

The rolls of roofing paper stripped from sheds and barn and carried to heaven knows where.

After an hour or so, the storm began to abate. The wind, which had ripped the top layers of bricks off the old farmhouse chimneys, no longer screeched so ferociously.

By evening, the storm passed, leaving an azure sky of brilliant beauty and an eerie calm.

The next day I walked down to Clark University where I was a sophomore. Woodland Street and Maywood Street and the other streets were almost impassable. Fallen trees were everywhere — on top of cars, smashed into roofs.

Dean Homer P. Little organized us into work crews to get the campus cleaned up. It took weeks before things were back to normal, but classes resumed in a day or two.

Back on the devastated farm, we bought a sawmill and for years cut lumber from the thousands of trees that had blown down on my father's various timberlots. There were so many excess logs at that time that they were dumped into ponds until they could be sawed up. They came in handy when World War II stimulated the demand for lumber in any shape or form.

Those are my recollections. They are not nearly as tragic as what happened to thousands of others. The 1938 hurricane killed more than 500 people in New England, mostly by drowning along the Rhode Island, Connecticut and Cape Cod coasts. Resort communities like Misquamicut were churned into a mass of wreckage, strewn with dead bodies. Thousands were injured. Thousands more lost heavily in property damage. About 20 Worcester County people lost their lives.

Property damage was estimated at $10 million. It probably was twice that. In Rhode Island, where damage was estimated at $100 million or more, 5,000 WPA workers were pressed into service to help bring things back to normal.

Like the coastal communities, river towns and cities suffered terribly. The water stood 20 feet deep in the middle of Ware. Barre Plains was one huge pond. Putnam, Conn., was ripped and ravaged by the swollen Quinapoxet. Winchendon was smashed and drenched. Churches everywhere lost their steeples. Worcester's First Unitarian Church, built in 1851, looked as if a bomb had hit it. Only the pillared portico was left relatively undamaged.

The havoc was wrought by a combination of rain and wind the like of which New England had never seen. More than four inches of rain fell on Sept. 20 and 21, and winds up to 115 mph were clocked.

September 1938 was a turning point for New England. Until then, people in these parts thought they were exempted from such things as hurricanes and tornadoes. Those happened elsewhere — in Florida, Louisiana and Oklahoma, for example.

Another hurricane, not so severe, hit the region in 1944. The Worcester tornado struck in 1953, and hurricanes Diane and Carol two and three years later.

Our time of innocence and invulnerability was over — gone with the shrieking wind.

Library of Congress

154

Chapter 35

Into the Light After 115 Years

ON A SUNNY DAY IN MAY 1968, Salvatore Virgilio was on his backhoe digging up history on the Worcester Common.

As he gingerly guided his scoop through the gravelly fill, a slight scraping sound caused him to hold up his hand in a gesture of caution.

Slowly the overlay was stripped away by the machine, and then by a man with a hand shovel. A photographer brushed away the last traces of dirt with a broom and took a picture. Only then was the old gravestone carefully lifted out and placed gently on the grass as the generations rolled away:

SACRED
To the
Memory of
Dr. Thomas Nichols
who died Dec. 9th
1794 in the 83rd
year of his age
Friends and physicians could not save
My mortal body from the grave
Nor can the grave confine me here
When Christ shall call me to appear

Much has been written about the digging up of the old burying ground on the Common. Anyone who was there to watch it felt a sense of awe and history. The old stones had lain buried for 115 years, by order of the Worcester City Council in 1853. In 1968, unearthed, they gave the modern city a glimpse of the remote past.

The Common has been here almost from the start of the third settlement in 1713. In those days it extended north to what is now Foster Street. It was a piece of land set aside for common ownership — a place where cattle and sheep grazed and where the meetinghouse and animal pound were built. By 1968, when the Common was elegantly redesigned, there was nothing in sight to recall the days

155

When Worcester had a Graveyard on the Common.

BRIERLY

AS YOU ARE NOW SO ONCE WAS I

Tombstones once dotted the eastern end of the Common. Near the present site of the Bigelow Monument and extending along Salem Square was WORCESTER'S SECOND BURIAL GROUND, 1730. It was enclosed by a stone wall with a gateway on the west side. From 1795, it fell into a state of sad neglect; the old wall was pulled down and the stones used for paving Main St. Finally, in 1850, all the grave stones were sunk a foot below the surface, over the occupants, and the whole grounds levelled off. Thus an old landmark passed from view. Among those buried here were Absolom Rice, son of Worcester's first permanent settler, John Chandler and Rev. Thaddeus Mac Carty, pastor of Old South Church for 37 years.

Worcester Telegram & Gazette

156

when Worcester was a tiny farming settlement under the rule of King George I of England. The oldest building near the Common in 1968 probably was the Salem Covenant Church (formerly a Baptist Church), dating from the mid-19th century, and that was torn down to make way for Worcester Center. The oldest structure on the Common itself was the Timothy Bigelow Monument, built during the Civil War.

Until 1853, the east end of the Common was a graveyard where the early settlers were buried. The place looked much different then. The Norwich and Worcester Railroad tracks ran straight across the Common. It was a familiar sight to see the smoke-belching engine, whistle tooting, heading for the Foster Street depot with its open cars rattling behind.

Old South Church and the old City Hall filled up the Main Street end of the Common. The east and north sides of the Common were an unsightly clutter.

In a reminiscence published by the Worcester Society of Antiquity a century ago, Nathaniel Paine reminisced on what the Common looked like in 1840 or thereabouts:

"The burial ground, situated at the east end of the Common, surrounded by a low stone wall, had an entrance on the west end; and on the north side were the tombs of the Wheeler and Dix families. This old ground was given up for burial purposes many years ago, and those grave stones which were not removed were laid flat and covered with earth and sods . . .

"On the southeast corner of the Common there stood for many years a one-story wooden school house, with a cupola and bell, which was used when I was a school boy, for the South Boys' Primary School . . . At one time it was used for the evening school for apprentices, which was afterwards kept in the lower town hall."

The Common in 1840, said Paine, was a much different place than it was in 1884. "It was here that the county cattle shows were held. Four rows of pens for the exhibition of cattle, swine and sheep, were put up on the north side, near Front Street, and extending from the Norwich railroad track nearly to where the Soldiers' Monument now is. The rest of the Common was given up to booths for the sale of refreshment of various kinds; and auctioneers' wagons, from which they sold whips, dry goods, soap and cheap jewelry. Cheap jacks traveled about the Common and streets adjacent, selling toothache drops, razors, gilt rings, and numerous articles to tempt the rural visitor. Often there would be tents pitched on the Common for the exhibition of monstrosities of various kinds, such as a two-headed calf, a mammoth horse or ox, fat girls, etc. Across Front street, west of where the track of the Norwich railroad used to be, was an open space extending to Mechanic street, which was filled with stands for the sale of sheet ginger-

Top: Charles Bouley and Daniel A. Farber check the gravestone of Elizabeth Jennison. Bottom left: The first gravestone uncovered in 1965 was that of Deacon Jacob Chamberlain. Bottom right: The headstone of Mrs. Sarah Tanner, who died on Sept. 19, 1785.

158

bread, cake, pies and confectionery, sweet cider and root beer. Here would be heard the loud call of the hot oyster man, to 'walk up, tumble up, any way to get up, and buy a bowl of hot oysters,' — very hot indeed, but with very few oysters."

Long before Summer's World, the Common was a lively place, a real center for community activity. But in 1840, the old graveyard was a link with the town's beginnings.

When they buried the old gravestones in 1853, the link was lost. It was not reforged until 1968, when 22 of the stones were placed in the small graveyard around the Timothy Bigelow Monument.

Time passes quickly. Even 1968 fades. But those messages on slate still speak. On the stone of Capt. Daniel Ward is inscribed:

> Now I behold with sweet delight
> The Blessed Three in one
> And Strange affections fix my sights
> On God's Incarnet son

And on that of Mrs. Irena Wiswell:

> Corruption, earth & worms
> Will but refine this flesh
> Until my spirit comes again
> And puts it on afresh

When the first of those old stones were erected around 1730, Worcester was a village of perhaps 400 persons. Pleasant Street was a lane. Paths and cart roads led to the small settlements in Oxford, Leicester, Charlton, Mendon and Brookfield. People still remembered the tales of the bloody Indian attacks that had destroyed the first two settlements in 1674 and 1684-89.

Those dark stones slowly bleaching in the May sunshine of 1968 pricked the imagination. For a moment, the sound of the traffic on Front and Franklin streets gave way to the clop-clop of horses' hooves, the cries of "cheap jacks" hawking wares, the shouts of ox drovers and the creaking sounds of wagons and chaises rolling along the dirt roads.

The link with the past had been reforged.

Worcester Telegram & Gazette

By the 1870s and 1880s, architects and contractors were learning how to build large buildings up to 12 stories high. Many mistakes were made in regard to fire and safety. The Chase Building was one of the biggest buildings that had been built in Worcester at that time.

160

Chapter 36

Two Old Dinosaurs Come Back to Life

*I*N 1984 AND 1985, two of Worcester's old dinosaurs got new leases on life. Their arteries had been clogged and they were well on the way to fossilization, but thanks to ingenious provisions in the federal tax laws, they were brought back to pristine condition.

One was the Day Building on Main Street and the other the Chase Building on Front Street. Both have interesting histories.

The Chase building was the pride of Ransom C. Taylor, Worcester's second-richest man in the late 19th century. He put up the massive structure in 1886 and named it for his wife, a member of the Chase family of Sutton. It may have cost $1 million. (In 1984, Rosewood Development of Framingham began to renovate the big building into a modern office block at an estimated eventual cost of $8 million.)

The "Taylor Block," as it was called when ground was broken a century ago, caused a lot of comment right from the start. It was the biggest building ever built in Worcester up to that time. It also was constructed on different principles than usual. Instead of inside load-bearing partitions made out of brick or stone, it had iron columns. Early on, some sidewalk supervisors wondered if it was safe.

According to the Worcester Daily Telegram of July 16, 1886:

"In the first place, the ground of criticism rests on the fact that the new Chase building is supported wholly on iron and steel pillars, and is devoid of brick partitions above the first floor. In case of fire in the building the question would be, how much heat would be required to warp and displace these columns?"

The industrious reporter sought out Fire Chief C.E. Combs for his opinion.

"I am not prepared to condemn the building," said the chief, "and I hear there is a story circulating that if a fire should start inside that building and make headway before the department arrived, I would refuse to allow any of the firemen to enter the building. I shall treat that building just the same as any other, and should do all in my power, with the fire department, to put out a fire. What I do say with reference to the Chase block is this: The building is dangerous as a fire risk."

161

The chief doubtless remembered another Taylor building that had gone up in a horrendous conflagration a few years before. That was the huge, five-story Taylor's Granite Building, built in 1871 across Main Street from where City Hall now stands. On May 28, 1875, a man working late in an upholstery establishment on the fourth floor carelessly dropped a lighted match. The dust, lint, pieces of cloth and waste burst into flame that virtually destroyed the building in a few hours, despite the best efforts of the Worcester and Leicester fire companies. No one was hurt, but the property damage was in the hundreds of thousands of dollars.

What worried Combs about the Chase Building was the iron pillars and the lack of supporting brick partitions. "When once thoroughly heated and the water strikes them, they are bound to crack and crumble, and then down will come the whole structure."

He had a suggestion: "Now my own idea is to have all these hollow columns kept constantly filled with running water, and in the case of fire the pillars would be sure to stand."

Worcester Telegram & Gazette

The Day Building was plagued with fires and problems. Yet it stands today, completely modernized and elegant.

162

Mr. Delano, the supervising architect, was not amused. The Chase building, he asserted, "is precisely the same as Clark's block (Denholm's) on Main Street, except that the latter is divided by a brick partition running to the roof." Anyway, he said, "there is no such thing as a fire-proof building in Worcester, and the Chase building is one of the best and the finest everyway that there is in the city."

Delano denied that the iron columns were hollow. They were filled with plaster of paris, he said, a fine non-conductor of heat. The square columns in the front were filled with brick.

When a "master mechanic" predicted that the iron columns would shrink by five feet, seven inches, Delano labeled the notion absurd. "The pillars and vaults are all set solidly in iron, and shrinkage is absolutely out of the question."

Despite the gossip, space in the building was much sought after. Even in July 1886, with construction still going on, "A large portion of the building has already been spoken for, and will be occupied as soon as completed," reported the Telegram.

When it was finished, the Chase building was topped by a Norman-type tower that loomed over Front Street and the Common. The tower has since been removed.

For generations, the big block was a beehive of activity. But after World War II, the upper floors gradually were abandoned to storage and warehouses or just plain emptiness. It was bought in February 1984 by Rosewood Development and partners. Shortly thereafter, the lights went on on all seven floors as the work crews moved in, hammering, pounding, sawing and ripping.

The renovated building meets all modern fire codes. Curiously, for all of Combs' doubts a century ago, the Chase Building seems to have had few problems. Research fails to uncover a single major fire at the building in the past century. The iron columns, opened up to the light a century after they were installed, still stood firm and unshrunken.

The Day Building, which was revamped into an elegant office building in 1984 by Cutler Associates, was not so lucky. During that renovation, the designers scratched their heads more than once. According to an article in The Evening Gazette by Christopher H. Schmitt, parts of a supporting column were missing and an inside wall was not precisely where it should have been.

It's not surprising, considering what the Day Building and its various annexes have been through since 1897, when John E. Day opened it for business.

It has been ravaged by major fires four times — in 1897, 1902, 1914 and 1918. No other big Worcester building can equal that record.

The first and worst of the conflagrations hit on March 5, 1897, when the Day Building was brand new. The Worcester Telegram reported that losses added up

163

to more than $300,000. Nine firemen were hurt in the general alarm fire and the building was described as a "complete wreck."

Day said he was covered by insurance and would rebuild the block immediately, which he did.

Five years later the Day Building annex was swept again by fire. That fire wiped out the property and plant of the Worcester Spy and marked the beginning of the end for that famed old newspaper. The Spy expired for good two years later.

The Telegram reported that losses were estimated at about $152,000. Day said he would rebuild, and he did.

On Oct. 16, 1914, the top two floors of the main Day Building were swept by fires that caused $150,000 damage, according to the Telegram. It reported that "a score of explosions" endangered firefighters and the thousands of spectators who lined the streets.

The Telegram reported that "the firefighters found a difficult task" when they entered the building. "The building is filled with studios and halls and is a maze to the stranger." But after the third alarm, 19 hose wagons, six trucks and six engines were playing 19 streams of water on the burning hulk.

Once again, the building was rebuilt.

The final Day building blaze came on April 4, 1918, when an annex on Eden Street caught fire. The flames ripped through the back part of the building and annex. When the Telegram reporter arrived, he saw "smoke pouring through the crevices and flames eating through the top of the door on the Walnut Street side." That fire almost claimed a victim, a girl who was sleeping in her fourth-floor apartment. She jumped out of a window and crashed through a skylight on an adjoining building.

That fire's damage toll was estimated at $150,000.

The building was rebuilt again, apparently with more attention paid to fire prevention. It has not been hit by a major fire since World War I.

Curiously, for all the destruction, the Day Building looks much the same on the outside as it did almost a century ago. Irwin Regent, who did the redesign, says that the building is one of the few examples of "Romanesque revival architecture" in Worcester.

That's good to know. Some might wonder whether it qualifies as a Neroesque revival building, given its past. It surely rates a special niche in the annals of Worcester fires.

164

Chapter 37

The Man Who Mastered Lincoln Square

*I*N APRIL 1970, a new television program called "It Couldn't Be Done" provided a bit of nostalgia for some Worcester viewers.

In a sequence depicting the great tunnels, particularly the Holland Tunnel under the Hudson River between New York and New Jersey, there was a shot of Ole Singstad shortly before his death in December 1970, at the age of 87.

There once again was the marvelous lilting Scandinavian brogue, the twinkling eyes, the gentle smile that often played over Singstad's face. With dramatic tunnel shots in the background, he described the problems of ventilating the Holland Tunnel back there in the 1920s, and of digging through the rock and mud 100 feet below the murky water.

Singstad's monument is underground all over the world. He was the Bach, Beethoven and Brahms of tunnel building. Name a major tunnel in Europe or America and Singstad probably had a hand in building it. In this country, besides the Holland Tunnel, he was the presiding genius over the construction of the first two tubes of the Lincoln Tunnel, the Baltimore Harbor tunnel, the Callahan Tunnel in Boston, the Ford Lauderdale New River Tunnel in Florida, the West Virginia Memorial Tunnel in Wheeling and the Intercoastal Waterway Tunnel in Houma, La.

Plus dozens more, too small to name. Those include the two tunnels at Worcester's own Lincoln Square.

Persons born after 1940 can hardly imagine what Lincoln Square used to be like in the rush hour — or even at ordinary times during the day or night. Some think the old rotary was bad, but the rotary was a piece of cake compared to what the square was when Singstad first laid eyes on it in 1952.

Back in earlier times, Lincoln Square was just a meadow where various paths crossed. Isaiah Thomas had an orchard nearby. The first and second Stephen Salisburys lived in the mansion then located where the Boys Club is now. It was moved up the hill in 1932, to make way for the new Memorial Auditorium.

Mill Brook then ran right through Lincoln Square. It was spanned by a short

165

OLE SINGSTAD

Above: Lincoln Square as it looked, circa 1880. It looked much the same when the great Norwegian engineer, Ole Singstad, took it in hand in the 1950s.

Worcester Telegram & Gazette

166

bridge, but the wetlands often flooded, making it hard for Salisbury, Thomas and everyone else to get from one side to the other. Years later, when the Blackstone Canal was built, the brook was buried underground in a huge conduit built of rocks. That conduit came to light briefly in the 1950s, when Hurricanes Carol and Diane forced a rebuilding of the storm sewer system from Lincoln Square south.

In the middle of the last century, the railroad was built through the square, where it was to remain the bane of cursing travelers for the next 100 years and more. People still recall the automobiles backed up in all directions as the signal gates came down and the 5 p.m. freight train made its leisurely way through. Horns tooted impatiently on Belmont, Summer, Main, Highland, Prescott, Salisbury, Union and Lincoln streets. More than one woman in labor gritted her teeth as she waited for the signals to go up so that she could be rushed to The Memorial Hospital. Fire engines were held up, sometimes for 10 minutes or more. It was a mess.

The city had talked about redesigning the square ever since the 1880s, but no one seemed to know how to solve the problem. Separating the east-west from the north-south traffic posed enormous difficulties in itself. In addition there was the railroad. No one had a clue as to what to do with it.

One plan, proposed by Gov. Paul Dever, would have bridged Lincoln Square by an overpass from Belmont Street to Highland Street. But that would have solved only part of the problem, besides being ugly.

What to do?

In a stroke of genius, the state Department of Public Works went to Ole Singstad. He was proof that it pays to hire the very best.

It did not take Singstad 15 minutes to figure out a basic plan. Run the railroad under Belmont Street ("made to order" for a tunnel) he told the fascinated City Council. Build a one-way north underpass from Main Street to Lincoln and Grove streets, take down some old buildings, build a big rotary around the square, reroute Summer Street to Lincoln Street by an underpass beneath Belmont Street, and install the necessary traffic lights and signs.

"Nothing to it," he assured the awed councilors in his singsong Scandinavian accent. "Nothing to it." He smiled benignly, like a kindly schoolmaster.

The City Council, awed by the legend before them in the flesh, hardly asked any questions. Without a dissenting vote, it adopted a radical new plan to solve a traffic knot that had tied up downtown Worcester for a century.

"If Ole built the Holland Tunnel," said Councilor James D. O'Brien, "he can take care of Lincoln Square all right."

Take care of it he did. The tunnels were built, precisely as he said. The railroad signal house disappeared. So did the signals. So did the trains. The rotary per-

167

Lincoln Square in the 1880s. The Salisbury Mansion stood where the Boys Club stands now. The Salisbury House can be seen at upper left.

A view from the north side of the square looking toward Union Street. Belmont Street is at extreme left.

168

formed well, especially in the early days before the traffic load reached the choke point. Drivers headed north on Main Street could whisk through the tunnel and be on Lincoln Street without even slowing down.

By 1980, with Worcester Center Boulevard on the drawing boards and all sorts of new construction planned and underway, a new traffic plan for Lincoln Square became a must. It opened in 1983, a considerable improvement over the rotary.

But the new plan owes much to the genius of Ole Singstad, too. Thanks to his train tunnel, the trains pass by unseen and unnoticed. Traffic flow in his other tunnel has been reversed and now carries traffic south instead of north under the square, but it still keeps hundreds of cars out of the square every day.

So, the next time you travel through Lincoln Square, give a thought to Ole Singstad, master tunnel builder. When all others despaired of a solution, he touched Lincoln Square with his magic wand.

And, lo, the traffic moved.

Worcester Historical Museum

Another view, looking north. The armory is at far left, the railroad signal house at right.

169

About the Author

ALBERT B. SOUTHWICK, newsman and historian, grew up in Leicester on the family farm, attended local schools and graduated from Clark University in 1941. He spent four years in the U.S. Navy during World War II, won his pilot's wings and did anti-submarine patrol off both coasts and from the Aleutian Islands. After the war, he received his M.A. in U.S. history from Clark University, did a year of study at Brown University and spent 1950-1952 as civilian historian for the U.S. Seventh Army, based in Stuttgart, Germany.

On returning from Germany, he worked as a reporter for the Providence Journal before becoming an editorial writer for the Worcester Telegram and Evening Gazette. From 1968 until his retirement in 1986, he was chief editorial writer for both papers.

He has written four books, "Once-Told Tales of Worcester County", More Once-Told Tales of Worcester County", "The Worcester Club at One Hundred Years" and "The Johnson Family of Hyde Park & Sag Harbor," plus many magazine and newspaper articles and stories.

He and his wife, Shirley live in Leicester. They have four children.